# The Pentateuch

A Liberation-Critical Reading of the Old Testament
Alice L. Laffey, Series Editor

*The Pentateuch*
Alice L. Laffey

*Israel's Wisdom Literature: A Liberation-Critical Reading*
Dianne Bergant

Forthcoming Volumes:
*The Deuteronomic History*
Sharon Pace Jeansonne

*The Prophets*
Carol Dempsey

# The Pentateuch

## A Liberation-Critical Reading

**Alice L. Laffey**

**Fortress Press**
**Minneapolis**

THE PENTATEUCH
A Liberation-Critical Reading

Scripture quotations from the New Revised Standard Version of the Bible are copyright © 1989 by the Division of Christian Education of the National Council of Churches of Christ in the United States of America and are used by permission.

Cover and book design by Joseph Bonyata.
Cover art by Sandra Bowden. Used by permission.

Library of Congress Cataloging in Publication Data
Laffey, Alice L.
    The Pentateuch : a liberation-critical reading / Alice L. Laffey.
    p.    cm.
    Includes bibliographical references and index.
    ISBN 0-8006-2872-1
    1. Bible. O.T. Pentateuch—Feminist criticism.  2. Liberation Theology.  I. Title.
BV1225.2.L34    1998
222'.106'082—dc21                      98–18082
                                                      CIP

The paper used in this publication meets the minimum requirements of American National Standard for Information Sciences—Permanence of Paper for Printed Library Materials, ANSI Z329.48-1984. ∞ ™

Manufactured in the U.S.A.                        AF 1-2872

02    01    00    99    98    1    2    3    4    5    6    7    8    9    10

# Contents

# Introduction

## About the Series

THIS FOUR-VOLUME SERIES of liberation-critical readings arose out of feminist concerns, including the conviction that the biblical texts were produced by men in a patriarchal culture, and that the ways in which the texts depict women and men are consequently conditioned by the assumptions associated with patriarchy. But such concerns lead to other concerns. If the culture depicted in the texts is patriarchal, then it is also hierarchical; its organization of society not only places men over women, but also places free men over slaves, rich over poor, and Israelite over foreigner, as if persons could be relegated to one rung of a ladder—and valued accordingly—depending on their sex, ethnic identity, or economic status. According to ladder-like or triangular models of social organization, even the humans on the lowest rung rank higher than nonhumans, with those living nonhumans commonly identified as animals ranking higher than those living nonhumans commonly identified as plants. According to this scheme, all living beings rank higher than the nonliving matter contained in the universe and of which the universe is composed.

Studies of the development of patriarchy in the ancient Near East suggest that its origins lie in the movement from a hunting to an agricultural society and in health crises that prompted the people to protect their pregnant women, and then to accentuate

1

women's role as mothers to the exclusion of their other contributions to society. What this development suggests is that patriarchy was not always extant, that it is not essential to the nature of the cosmos.

The men who produced the texts we refer to today as the Hebrew Scriptures or the Old Testament did, in fact, accept the patriarchal/hierarchical paradigm. We can assume, therefore, that they ranked humans over nonhumans and living nonhumans over those elements of the universe they experienced as nonliving. Yet the expressions of patriarchy prevalent in the ancient Near East did not coincide with the many manifestations with which we are familiar today. In the intervening three thousand years humans have been seeking to conquer and control their surroundings in order to place everything, including some human beings, at the disposal of other human beings. To a deceiving extent humans have succeeded in taming nature, harnessing natural resources, controlling data, reaching superpower status, and achieving economic dominance.

The distance between 1000 B.C.E. and 2000 C.E. is great, and much has transpired during those years to separate what the writers of the biblical texts understood as they wrote from what contemporary readers understand when they read. This is true not only of the texts that depict women, but also of the biblical literature that describes nature. Though the ancient Israelites may have wished to conquer and control their environment—after all, they lived with the constant threat of drought and famine, pestilence and plague—they, in contrast to many of us, experienced keenly that they were not in control. They experienced a close relationship with animals and food-bearing plants. The peoples of the ancient Near East sought the favor of powers higher than themselves, the blessings of fertility gods, or of "the God who brought us up out of Egypt"; they looked to these higher powers to provide those things on which they depended for continued survival but which they could not control: the rain and sunshine so desperately needed for the harvest and the fertility of their animals.

The modern consciousness no longer looks to higher powers to control nature but, rather, believes that humankind has been endowed with the power to control nature. Because much of nature has been brought under human control, human beings sometimes think that total control is possible: it is only a matter of time and increased technology. Such a consciousness assumes the hierarchical paradigm, the appropriateness of dominion. Yet, truth be told, humankind has not successfully conquered or controlled its surroundings, in spite of feverish efforts over the last three thousand years. During those years humankind has moved from a relationship of respect toward the power of nature to resenting its power, and working toward its domination. Assuming the appropriateness of the hierarchical paradigm, humans have sought to move higher on the rungs of the ladder, displacing the gods, and relegating to lower and lower rungs the less powerful—the nonhuman and the nonliving elements of creation. Because it is easier to dominate and destroy that which is experienced as inferior, as life-threatening or evil, than that which is experienced as equal or superior—before which one stands in awe and respect—the hierarchical paradigm has consistently sought to devalue nature.

Yet this has been done at enormous cost—to humankind and to the environment. At present, ecologists warn that an irreversible process has been initiated that already is destroying the ecosystem. Though some have begun to lament the accretion of nuclear waste and the depletion of the ozone layer, large-scale conservation projects have not been implemented, and the raping of the rain forests continues.

A feminist consciousness that assumes a nonhierarchical paradigm, that does not seek to achieve and/or maintain superiority, but that promotes equality, mutuality, and reciprocity between the sexes, also commits itself to peace, to empowering those human persons whom the hierarchical social organization has relegated to its lower rungs, the human persons whom society considers less powerful and who are therefore potentially more vulnerable (in First World societies, the elderly, racial minorities, gays and lesbians, the poor), and to fostering respect for and cooperation with all nonhuman participants in and inhabitants of the cosmos.

The period in which the biblical texts were produced was a time when the living and nonliving elements of the universe functioned in closer relationship than they do in most parts of the First World today. Humankind tilled the soil and depended on that soil to bring forth fruit; for its part, the soil depended on rain. Dependence and sparsity led naturally to conservation. Dependence on nature, which showed the Israelites they were not in control, and dependence on the gods who controlled nature—when combined with reaping the benefits of nature, the prosperity associated with fertility of animals and crops—produced among the Israelites a relationship with nature very different from our own. They were able to balance their fear of nature and of its unpredictability and potential devastation with a deep appreciation for its bounty, and for the gods who provided the bounty.

This balance of nature's blessings and curses lies behind descriptions of nature in the biblical texts. Because nature could not be controlled by human beings, human beings could not take it for granted. The balance between benefit and harm which the writers experienced and articulated and which moderns, so intent on domination, have frequently failed to experience in reading the texts resonates throughout. At a time when humankind is learning again that it is not in control, at a time when we are beginning to realize the mixed blessings arising from our efforts to control, we cannot afford to read the biblical texts and continue to assume the legitimacy of the hierarchical paradigm.

This series of liberation-critical readings is divided into four parts, conforming roughly to the traditional sections of the Bible, the Pentateuch, the Historical Books, the Prophetic Literature, and the Wisdom Literature. Each volume assumes that patriarchy and hierarchy are not products of divine will but of human social organization. Although the Bible has been written and interpreted according to the patriarchal paradigm, this paradigm is becoming epistemologically suspect; new avenues for reading the texts must emerge. In keeping with respect for diversity, the volumes differ in their style of presentation. Nevertheless, they share and are governed by these assumptions.

A liberation-critical methodology uses traditional historical and literary methodologies but may transcend them. It assumes the relevance for interpretation of the historical and social worlds of the texts' origins, to the extent that it is possible to retrieve them. It assumes also that we have literary texts, now existing independently of the authors who produced them. No matter what the original authors intended to communicate, the texts are interpreted by those who read them. Further, the method assumes that readers bring to interpretation their own understandings of the world; these understandings are invariably influenced by the historical period and the social context in which these readers live as well as by their personal histories and experiences. Finally, a liberation-critical methodology assumes a nonhierarchical paradigm and consequently seeks to emphasize those texts and interpretations which are believed to be liberating, freeing, and life-giving. In these volumes, liberation-critical interpretations are meant to be just that—liberating, freeing, and life-giving—for all of the components of creation that stand in relationship to one another.

## About This Volume

In this volume of the series I hope to highlight the interdependence of all the individual characters and types of characters portrayed in the Pentateuch: God, human beings, animals, plants, and elements. To that end, the comments, while making every effort not to distort a narrative or teaching, deliberately, wherever possible, accentuate the nonhuman, since modern readers are almost always accustomed to reading the texts through the lens of human and divine interaction. For this reason characters such as water, trees, camels, and sheep appear in certain subtitles.

The volume has been developed in eight chapters. Part one (chapters 1–3), beginning with creation, comments on pentateuchal texts that illustrate the essential relationships among nonhuman, divine, and human characters: "Cosmic and Human Interdependence" (chapter 1); that affirm the appropriate relationship of humans to nature and to each other: "Use, Not Abuse" (chapter 2); and that attest to the critical role of secure land for creation's, especially a people's, survival: "The Land, a Promised Treasure" (chapter 3).

Part two (chapters 4–5) focuses on improper power relations—abuse and domination—and assumes human beings' responsibility for sin. Chapter 4 examines the paradigmatic domination of human beings by other human beings, women by men, under the heading, "Sin: The Legitimation of Patriarchy." Chapter 5 comments on texts that depict other forms of domination and subjugation of some human beings by others, including women by women and men by men, as well as abuses by human beings that involve nonhuman elements of creation, under the heading, "Sin: the Legitimation of Hierarchy."

Part three (chapters 6–8) contains text and commentary that moves from sin to deliverance and restores right relationship among all the elements of God's creation. Slavery is one expression of distorted power relations; the Israelites' deliverance from slavery—made possible by the collaboration of many human and non-human elements of God's creation—provides the biblical material commented on in "Liberation" (chapter 6). The liberation depicted is *for* covenant relationship. "Belonging: Covenantal Relationship" comments on texts that highlight the special relationship of the liberated people with God; belonging transcends the alienation of sin (chapter 7). Finally, "Reciprocity" reflects on biblical texts that demonstrate attitudes and behaviors appropriate to those liberated and in covenant relationship (chapter 8).

Most, though not all, of the texts of the Pentateuch are examined here. By reordering the texts according to a conceptual framework that highlights the interdependence (chapter 1) and reciprocity (chapter 8) that the biblical texts themselves exhibit, the volume hopes to increase the reader's consciousness of the relationships of mutuality and respect that the writers of the biblical materials possessed and to which the readers of the biblical texts today are called.

# 1

# Cosmic and Human Interdependence

## Creation Stories

THERE HAVE BEEN AT LEAST THREE approaches to the interpretation of Genesis 1–2 during the past century: (1) a scientific emphasis which focuses on the meaning of the Hebrew words *tōhû wābōhû*, the "formlessness and void" out of which, according to the narrative, God created; (2) a historical-critical emphasis, which separates the two chapters into two sources and determines that Gen. 1:1—2:4a is the product of a Priestly source and Gen. 2:4b-25, the product of the Yahwist source; (3) a feminist emphasis which stresses God's creating *'ādām*—"male and female he created them" (Gen. 1:27)—and that *'ādām*, created alone, needed a "helpmate fit for him" (Gen. 2:18). These emphases contrast with earlier tradition, which used the texts to legitimate man's understanding of himself as superior to woman and man's efforts to dominate the earth (1:28). I intend to suggest that Gen. 1:28 balances the previous verses and thus places humans in an interdependent relationship with nature.

### Genesis 1:1—2:4a

(1:1) In the beginning when God created the heavens and the earth, (2) the earth was a formless void and darkness covered the face of the deep, while a wind from God swept over the face of the waters.

Verse 1 equates the heavens and the earth with the first act of creation, and attributes that creation to the action of God. A description of the earth follows; at that time it was a formless void. There was darkness (no light); there was water, its movement made possible by wind; the wind, too, was from God.

The heavens, the earth, darkness, water, and wind—none of these aspects of God's creation depends on humanity for its continued existence.

> (3) Then God said, "Let there be light"; and there was light. (4) And God saw that the light was good; and God separated the light from the darkness. (5) God called the light Day, and the darkness he called Night. And there was evening and there was morning, the first day.

Light, which is absolutely essential for life, had to exist before, or at least simultaneously with, plant and animal life. Without light all living things die; therefore, all living things depend on light for their very existence.

> (6) And God said, "Let there be a dome in the midst of the waters, and let it separate the waters from the waters." (7) So God made the dome and separated the waters that were under the dome from the waters that were above the dome. And it was so. (8) God called the dome Sky. And there was evening and there was morning, the second day.

Rainwater, the water that comes from above, is absolutely essential to the life and growth of plants, without which animals, including humans, could not survive.

> (9) And God said, "Let the waters under the sky be gathered together in one place, and let the dry land appear." And it was so. (10) God called the dry land Earth, and the waters that were gathered together he called Seas. And God saw that it was good.

The waters of the oceans, the lakes, and the rivers are essential to the life of algae, fish, and so forth. Without the water that they inhabit, these creatures would not be able to survive. Without water to drink, coming from below as well as from above, animals, including humans, could not survive. On the other hand, without dry land most animals could not breathe and would die.

> (11) Then God said, "Let the earth put forth vegetation: plants yielding seed, and fruit trees of every kind on earth that bear fruit with the seed in it." And it was so. (12) The earth brought forth vegetation: plants yielding seed of every kind, and trees of every kind bearing fruit with the seed in it. And God saw that it was good. (13) And there was evening and there was morning, the third day.

With darkness and light, dry land and water in place, the earth is able to bear plant life. And plant life—fruits and vegetables—produces seed, the wherewithal to reproduce. Without fruits and vegetables, many animals, including humans, either could not live at all or, at best, would not be healthy.

> (14) And God said, "Let there be lights in the dome of the sky to separate the day from the night; and let them be for signs and for seasons and for days and years, (15) and let them be lights in the dome of the sky to give light upon the earth." And it was so. (16) God made the two great lights—the greater light to rule the day and the lesser light to rule the night—and the stars. (17) God set them in the dome of the sky to give light upon the earth, (18) to rule over the day and over the night, and to separate the light from the darkness. And God saw that it was good. (19) And there was evening and there was morning, the fourth day.

For the author of Genesis 1 morning and evening, darkness and light precede the creation of the sun, the moon, and the stars. For the ancients the sun did not always shine, nor were the moon and stars always present to lighten the darkness of the night. They were therefore experienced as less essential to the survival of plant life than were evening and morning, light and dark. As the text indicates, the sun, moon, and stars shed light on the earth, and they enabled a sense of direction and the calculation of longer periods of time.

> (20) And God said, "Let the waters bring forth swarms of living creatures, and let birds fly above the earth across the dome of the sky." (21) So God created the great sea monsters and every living creature that moves, of every kind, with which the waters swarm, and every winged bird of every kind. And God saw that it was good. (22) God blessed them, saying, "Be fruitful and multiply and fill the waters in the seas, and let birds multiply on the earth." (23) And there was evening and there was morning, the fifth day.

With water "gathered together in one place" the rivers, lakes, and oceans could now support sea creatures—fish, sharks, crocodiles, and so forth. With sky separating the waters above from the waters below, dry land separated from the waters, and plants firmly in place, birds could fly through the sky, settle, eat and drink, and survive. And all these creatures—inhabitants of the waters and of the skies—were created with the potential to reproduce themselves.

> (24) And God said, "Let the earth bring forth living creatures of every kind: cattle and creeping things and wild animals of the earth of every kind." And it was so. (25) God made the wild animals of the earth of every kind, and the cattle of every kind, and everything that creeps upon the ground of every kind. And God saw that it was good.

These verses provide for the existence of animal life forms. Only when there is sunlight, dry land and water, rainfall and crops, can animals survive. Only into a world where such things already existed, a world that today might be described as having its "infrastructure in place," could animals come and survive.

> (26) Then God said, "Let us make humankind in our image, according to our likeness; and let them have dominion over the fish of the sea, and over the birds of the air, and over the cattle, and over all the wild animals of the earth, and over every creeping thing that creeps upon the earth." (27) So God created humankind in his image, in the image of God he created them; male and female he created them. (28) God blessed them, and God said to them, "Be fruitful and multi-

ply, and fill the earth and subdue it; and have dominion over
the fish of the sea and over the birds of the air and over
every living thing that moves upon the earth." (29) God
said, " See, I have given you every plant yielding seed that is
upon the face of all the earth, and every tree with seed in its
fruit; you shall have them for food. (30) And to every beast
of the earth, and to every bird of the air, and to everything
that creeps on the earth, everything that has the breath of
life, I have given every green plant for food." And it was so.
(31) God saw everything that he had made, and indeed, it
was very good. And there was evening and there was morning, the sixth day.

The phrases "in our image," "according to our likeness" (1:26)
have alternated with the verbs "subdue" and "have dominion
over" as major points of emphasis in the exegesis of these verses.
Humankind, it has been stressed, is superior to all the other elements of creation because it has been created "in the likeness of
God." Furthermore, in contrast to other creatures, its role is to
have dominion over other creatures—over all the fish, birds, cattle, wild animals, and creeping things—and to "subdue the earth."
A closer look at the text in 1:26-31, however, reveals the possibility of different and complementary interpretations. In what
ways are human beings created to be like God? Are they, like God,
to determine that all the elements of creation are good? Are they,
like God, to work—even to create? Is the author of the text here
legitimating power for human beings just as God has power? Then
one must ask, how is God's power used?
Up to this point in the narrative nothing has been said about
the destruction of some elements so that other elements of creation can survive. God separated light from darkness; God did not
destroy darkness to create light. God separated the waters above
from the waters below; God did not destroy any water in order to
create the sky. God separated the waters below from the dry land;
God did not destroy any water to create the dry land. Although
seed-bearing vegetation needs light and water to survive, it does
not destroy or diminish light or water, nor is the existence of sun,
moon, and stars understood to destroy (or even to diminish)

other elements of creation. It is obvious, however, that beasts, birds, creeping things—everything that breathes—needs food in order to live. It would also seem that, in these verses, provision is made for the nurturance of some elements of creation at the expense of (by the consumption of) others. Such feeding is portrayed as an act of domination, but domination that is legitimate. The domination (or consumption) of plant life—plants and fruit—is permitted in order that animals, including humans, can survive. The verse that legitimates human domination of fish, birds, cattle, wild animals, and creeping things may simply indicate that by the sixth century B.C.E. humankind used animals for farming and may have been carnivorous. Whereas certain elements of creation, once created, are self-sufficient, animals are not. They are not only dependent on other elements of creation (e.g., plants need sunlight), their existence depends on the use of (and perhaps the consumption of) others. To legitimate such domination, the author may well have found it necessary to compare humankind to God; only God could legitimately do—or legitimate what man needed to do—to effect human survival.

This interpretation does not intend to suggest that the author who produced these texts was not patriarchal; as a product of his culture, he undoubtedly was thoroughly hierarchical. What it does suggest, however, is that the ancients understood their relationship to nature very differently from how humans now understand that relationship, after three thousand years of "subduing" and "having dominion over" and legitimating that behavior with an explanation of our difference from other creatures. In fact, according to the narrative, all the animals including humans are created on the sixth day. The text has been interpreted as referring to human rationality—the ability to speak, to write, and to remember—but the text makes no mention of these qualities. Human beings continue to exaggerate the difference between themselves and other animals in spite of the fact that much is now known about the sophisticated intelligence—the memory, the ability to communicate, and so forth—of certain other animals.

(2:1) Thus the heavens and the earth were finished, and all their multitude. (2) And on the seventh day God finished the work that he had done, and he rested on the seventh day from all the work that he had done. (3) So God blessed the seventh day and hallowed it, because on it God rested from all the work that he had done in creation. (4a) These are the generations of the heavens and the earth when they were created.

The author of these verses here describes God anthropomorphically—God, like human beings, rests after working. This may account for why, according to Gen. 1:27, humankind is made "in the image of God." Moreover, the Priestly source responsible for this account of creation—also associated with the genealogies of the Pentateuch—uses the phrase "the generations of the heavens and the earth." When used to introduce genealogies, the term *generations* implies historical sequence and involves human personages. Used in this context, the term implies that creation involved an evolutionary process. In contrast to how the text is usually interpreted, this process was not a movement from simple to complex forms, but rather a movement from self-sustaining matter to more dependent life forms.

### Genesis 2:4b-25

Gen. 2:4b-25 is rarely considered on its own terms, as an account of creation. Rather, Gen. 2:4b—3:23 is examined together as one literary unit, and not without good reason. The tree of knowledge of good and evil, the tree of life, and humankind's nakedness are introduced in chapter 2 (vv. 9, 11, 17, and 25), but they play no part in the action of the narrative until chapter 3 (vv. 5, 7, 10-11, 22). If one takes Gen. 2:4b-25 as an independent literary unit, the tree of knowledge of good and the tree of life are merely two particular trees that God has created. Nakedness is simply a description by the text's author of how God had created humankind.

Historical criticism has shown that Genesis 2:4b—3:23 was probably produced by the Yahwist source in the early tenth century B.C.E. The Yahwist interpreted death, patriarchy, pain at childbirth, and work as consequences of humankind's disobedience to

God. The Israelites' earliest memories contained these hardships that humankind could not control, and so the Yahwist concluded that humankind's offense occurred shortly after humans were created. That is the most frequently accepted modern interpretation of the narrative presented in Genesis 3. But God's creating occurred before the harmony was disturbed, and it is to this part of the narrative that we wish to attend.

> (4b) In the day that the LORD God made the earth and the heavens, (5) when no plant of the field was yet in the earth and no herb of the field had yet sprung up—for the LORD God had not caused it to rain upon the earth, and there was no one to till the ground: (6) but a stream would rise from the earth, and water from the whole face of the ground—(7) then the LORD God formed a living creature ['ādām] from the dust of the ground ['ădāmāh] and breathed into his nostrils the breath of life; and the 'ādām became a living being.

The text describes the first stage of creation as the existence of heaven and earth. In that earliest stage there could be no plants and no herbs because as yet no rain had been created, nor had anyone been created who could or would till the soil. The text portrays plant life as dependent on rain water and, at least implicitly, on tilled earth, and, in turn, the tilled earth as dependent on someone to till it. According to this account, the first thing that God created—after heaven and earth (and the water that sprung from the earth)—was a living being, in Hebrew 'ādām, that God had formed out of the dust, the dry 'ădāmāh. The close relationship of the living creature to the ground is stressed by the wordplay, 'ādām from 'ădāmāh.

> (8) And the LORD God planted a garden in Eden, in the east; and there he put the man whom he had formed. (9) Out of the ground the LORD God made to grow every tree that is pleasant to the sight and good for food, the tree of life also in the midst of the garden, and the tree of the knowledge of good and evil.

The living creature God had made could not survive without food, so God provided, planting a garden that brought forth fruit and other trees. Just as plants and herbs could not survive without someone to till the ground, so the tiller could not survive without that which was tilled. Just as 'ādām stood in close relationship to 'ădāmāh, so the plants were dependent on the 'ādām for the tilling of the 'ădāmāh. The 'ādām, once created, was dependent on the fruit of the tilling of the ground, including trees God made to grow in the garden, for food. The extent of the interdependence is obvious.

> (10) A river flows out of Eden to water the garden, and from there it divides and becomes four branches. (11) The name of the first is Pishon; it is the one that flows around the whole land of Havilah, where there is gold; (12) and the gold of that land is good; bdellium and onyx stone are there. (13) The name of the second river is Gihon; it is the one that flows around the whole land of Cush. (14) The name of the third river is Tigris, which flows east of Assyria. And the fourth river is the Euphrates.

No garden can endure without water, and so God provided water in the form of a river; one thinks of fertile soil along banks of rivers. If more land is to be enriched by water, however, then more rivers are needed; thus the author describes the four directions, to the four corners of the earth, that is, to the ends of the earth. Some, though not all, of the land is rich in minerals and precious stones.

> (15) The LORD God took the man and put him in the garden of Eden to till it and keep it.

The 'ādām whom God had created God placed in the garden that God had created after the 'ādām, so that the 'ādām could take care of it. In this account of creation, 'ādām is needed to care for the ground so that trees (plants and herbs) can flourish.

> (16) And the LORD God commanded the man, "You may freely eat of every tree of the garden; (17) but of the tree of

the knowledge of good and evil you shall not eat, for in the day that you eat of it you shall die."

God speaks for the first time to 'ādām, providing for humankind's need for food. God has created many trees from which humankind may eat; however, humankind cannot eat from every tree. God established limits. Whereas most of the trees will sustain humankind's life, the forbidden tree will end it. Are we to conclude that humankind's life will continue to be nourished and never end if 'ādām does not eat from the forbidden tree (thereby incurring death as punishment)? Or do the verses presume that humankind will eventually die, although eating from a forbidden tree will precipitate an untimely and therefore unnatural death? The verses are in themselves ambiguous.

> (18) Then the LORD God said, "It is not good that the 'ādām should be alone; I will make him a helper as his partner."

This account of creation makes no provision (even implicit) for the perpetuation of the trees. Their fruit is assumed, in contrast to 'ādām's, perhaps because there are many of them. The Lord now wishes to create for 'ādām a helper fit as a partner. At this point in the narrative, one might conclude that God wishes to create for 'ādām another 'ādām who will help "till the ground and keep it," helping to nurture the trees that provide 'ādām's food.

> (19) So out of the ground the LORD God formed every animal of the field and every bird of the air, and brought them to the man to see what he would call them; and whatever the man called every living creature, that was its name. (20) The man gave names to all cattle, and to the birds of the air, and to every animal in the field; but for the man there was not found a helper as a partner.

Traditional interpretations have placed much emphasis on the function of 'ādām in naming, and certainly names given to human persons are significant in ancient Israel and in the texts of the Old Testament. Naming, however, does not have to imply control and superiority. Naming, in fact, can be affective and relational. Here the purpose of the naming seems to be to identify the creation, to differentiate among them and from 'ādām. They are creations of God different from, though no better than, 'ādām. 'Adām, created before them, names their identity, and since each is presented seemingly as a potential partner for 'ādām, 'ādām's naming is an articulation of relationship.

> (21) So the LORD God caused a deep sleep to fall upon man, and he slept; then he took one of his ribs and closed up its place with flesh. (22) And the rib that the LORD God had taken from the man he made into a woman and brought her to the man. (23) Then the man said, "This at last is bone of my bones and flesh of my flesh; this one shall be called Woman, for out of Man this one was taken."

Whereas God's other creatures were different from 'ādām, this new creation is taken from 'ādām, made out of the very stuff of 'ādām, more 'ādām than any other creation that God had created. 'Adām expresses this intimate connection by naming the new creation. One is 'îsh, man; the other, 'ishāh, woman. The names suggest that they are almost the same but not exactly the same. Their flesh and their bones are alike.

> (24) Therefore a man leaves his father and his mother and clings to his wife, and they become one flesh.

There is no father and mother in the narrative, the Yahwist source is very familiar with fathers and mothers, with population and children. Whereas God's other creations were not like 'ādām, there is now a way for there to be others like 'ādām.

> (25) And the man and his wife were both naked, and were not ashamed.

This verse provides a transition to chapter 3. "Naked" in Hebrew is ărûmmîm, whereas the serpent described in 3:1 is "cunning" ('ārûm). Like the tree of knowledge and the tree of life (2:17), the nakedness of humankind functions here as a literary foreshadowing of future events. The description is neutral at the least, or, when taken with their lack of shame, is a positive assertion of the openness of 'îsh and 'ishāh to each other.

# Salvific Wood, Conservation, and Destructive Water

## Valuing the Nonhuman (Gen. 6:5-13)

Much modern exegesis of Genesis 6–9 has concentrated either on the narrative's relationship to other ancient Near Eastern flood stories, most notably the Babylonian epic of Gilgamesh, or has been careful to separate the Yahwist and Elohist versions, noting frequent repetitions and seemingly glaring contradictions. Some attention, though slight, has been paid to the repetitive naming of the men in the narrative—Noah, Shem, Ham, Japheth—while the names of the women, the men's wives, are not mentioned. Hardly any attention has been paid to the nonhuman characters: earth and heaven; "all flesh," including nonhuman animals and birds; water, plants, and trees; and a raven and dove. The functions these characters perform are as integral to the narrative's development as the role of Noah. Because the contemporary reader is programmed to read and hear the narrative through the lens of its importance and application to humans, the following interpretation will deliberately minimize Noah's role in order to balance the reader's tendencies.

> (5) The Lord saw that the wickedness of humankind was great in the earth, and that every inclination of the thoughts of their hearts was only evil continually. (6) And the Lord was sorry that he had made humankind on the earth, and it grieved him to his heart. (7) So the Lord said, "I will blot out from the earth the human beings I have created—people together with animals and creeping things and birds of the air, for I am sorry that I have made them." (8) But Noah found favor in the sight of the Lord.

Wickedness and evil are associated with humankind—with their intentions if not their actions. As a consequence, God determines to destroy the animals—human and nonhuman—which God had created. Only one human—"but" introduces Noah as a contrast to other humans—"found favor" with God.

> (9) These are the descendants of Noah. Noah was a right-
> eous man, blameless in his generation; Noah walked with
> God. (10) And Noah had three sons, Shem, Ham, and
> Japheth.

Verses 9-10 explain why Noah found favor with God. In contrast to the wickedness and evil dominating his generation, Noah
represented righteousness and blamelessness. Noah has three
sons, a number often used symbolically in the Old Testament to
signify completion. The information provided in verse 10 foreshadows the narrative to follow.

> (11) Now the earth was corrupt in God's sight, and the
> earth was filled with violence. (12) And God saw that the
> earth was corrupt; for all flesh had corrupted its ways upon
> the earth. (13) And God said to Noah, "I have determined to
> make an end of all flesh, for the earth is filled with violence
> because of them; now I am going to destroy them along
> with the earth."

Whereas humankind had become evil, the earth had become
filled with violence; "all flesh" had been corrupted. This passage
obviously does not only indict humankind, but the earth itself
along with its animals—human and nonhuman—that God had
created. According to verse 7, God wished to blot out the nonhuman animals along with humankind, and now we know why. Corruption had come to characterize action, and violence controlled
relationship. With the dominance of such behavior God targeted
the earth and all flesh for destruction. Whereas God spoke without a specifically named audience in verse 7, God now directs his
condemnation to a particular person, Noah.

### Salvific Wood (Gen. 6:14-17)

> (14) "Make yourself an ark of cypress wood; make rooms in
> the ark, and cover it inside and out with pitch. (15) This is
> how you are to make it: the length of the ark three hundred
> cubits, its width fifty cubits, and its height thirty cubits. (16)
> Make a roof for the ark, and finish it to a cubit above; and
> put the door of the ark in its side; make it with lower, sec-

ond, and third decks. (17) For my part, I am going to bring
a flood of waters on the earth, to destroy from under heaven
all flesh in which is the breath of life; everything that is on
the earth shall die."

In a series of imperatives, God orders Noah to build a wooden
ark, specifying its size and how it is to be made. God then informs
Noah that God intends to flood the earth so that all living flesh—
human and nonhuman—will be destroyed.

### Conservation (Gen. 6:18—7:5)

(6:18) "But I will establish my covenant with you; and you
shall come into the ark, you, your sons, your wife, and your
sons' wives with you. (19) And of every living thing, of all
flesh, you shall bring two of every kind into the ark, to keep
them alive with you; they shall be male and female. (20) Of
the birds according to their kinds, and of the animals
according to their kinds, of every creeping thing of the
ground according to its kind, two of every kind shall come
in to you, to keep them alive. (21) Also take with you every
kind of food that is eaten, and store it up; and it shall serve
as food for you and for them." (22) Noah did this; he did all
that God commanded him.

In contrast to the other animals who would be destroyed, God
promised to establish a relationship with Noah to save him and his
family from the floodwaters. God likewise provided that a pair—
with the potential for procreation—of all the other animals
should be protected by the saving wood of Noah's ark. Finally, to
provide for those destined to survive, God instructed that all the
plants used for food should be stored in the ark. All that God told
Noah to do—building the ark, taking in male and female representatives of all flesh (human and nonhuman animals), storing
enough food to secure the survival of those destined to be saved—
these things Noah did.

(7:1) Then the LORD said to Noah, "Go into the ark, you and
all your household, for I have seen that you alone are righteous before me in this generation. (2) Take with you seven
pairs of all clean animals, the male and its mate; and a pair

of the animals that are not clean, the male and its mate; (3) and seven pairs of the birds of the air also, male and female, to keep their kind alive on the face of all the earth. (4) For in seven days I will send rain on the earth for forty days and forty nights; and every living thing that I have made I will blot out from the face of the ground." (5) And Noah did all that the LORD had commanded him.

God's command to Noah regarding himself, his family, and the animals and birds is now made explicit: go into the ark. The explanation for the rescue of Noah's family among all families of the earth is made more explicit: Noah is the only human among his generation whom God judges righteous. Gen. 7:1-5 orders Noah to take seven pairs of clean animals and birds, and only one pair of unclean animals, into the ark. Seven, like three, is frequently used in biblical texts to symbolize completion. The difference in the number of clean animals and birds (seven pairs) and unclean animals (one pair) may indicate that clean animals and birds could be used for food, or that clean animals had greater value. Taking one male and one female of each kind on board the ark indicates an emphasis on reproduction, but taking seven pairs allows for both consumption and offerings.

At God's appointed time—after seven days—God would send rain until it was appropriate for the rain to end. (The number forty designates the fullness of time.) The duration of the rain would be sufficient to destroy all that existed on the 'ădāmāh. Again the narrator reports that Noah obeyed the Lord: Noah entered the ark, taking his family and the other designated creatures with him.

### Destructive Water (Gen. 7:6—8:12)

(7:6) Noah was six hundred years old when the flood of waters came on the earth. (7) And Noah with his sons and his wife and his sons' wives went into the ark to escape the waters of the flood. (8) Of clean animals, and of animals that are not clean, and of birds, and of everything that creeps on the ground, (9) two and two, male and female, went into the ark with Noah, as God had commanded Noah. (10) And after seven days the waters of the flood came on the earth.

Noah is elderly, a blessing that comes to the righteous. Gen. 7:6-10 repeats verses 2-5 with little variation; instead of direct address, God telling Noah what to do, the narrator records what Noah did, that is, what the Lord commanded. The narrator records that God accomplished what was predicted, and the rains came. Gen. 7:6-10 appears to contradict the earlier count of animals Noah would take into the ark, indicating only one pair of each kind. Whether the variations in number of animals can be attributed to a different source, or whether in 7:2-3 one pair was to be preserved with the other pairs serving as food (or later offerings), is irrelevant to our emphasis. Provision was made for the preservation of every kind of living animal and bird on the earth.

> (7:11) In the six hundredth year of Noah's life, in the second month, on the seventeenth day of the month, on that day all the fountains of the great deep burst forth, and the windows of the heavens were opened. (12) The rain fell on the earth forty days and forty nights. (13) On the very same day Noah with his sons, Shem and Ham and Japheth, and Noah's wife and the three wives of his sons entered the ark, (14) they and every wild animal of every kind, and all domestic animals of every kind, and every creeping thing that creeps on the earth, and every bird of every kind—every bird, every winged creature. (15) They went into the ark with Noah, two and two of all flesh in which there was the breath of life. (16) And those that entered, male and female of all flesh, went in as God had commanded him; and the LORD shut him in.

A precise date—day, month, and year—for the beginning of the destructive floodwaters establishes the authenticity of the report. According to ancient cosmology, water existed both above and below the earth. Both of these water sources flooded the earth until it was time for the flood to end. That, according to this report, Noah, his family, and representatives of all flesh entered the ark on the day the rain began differs from verse 10, which seems to imply that they entered the ark seven days before the rain began. Whether this discrepancy can be attributed to different sources, or whether the author simply uses two numbers symbolic of completion (seven and one) to describe the same events, is unclear. In any case, the text reiterates that what took place accorded with the Lord's command to Noah. The Lord then closed the ark.

> (7:17) The flood continued forty days on the earth; and the waters increased, and bore up the ark, and it rose high above the earth. (18) The waters swelled and increased greatly on the earth; and the ark floated on the face of the waters. (19) The waters swelled so mightily on the earth that all the high mountains under the whole heaven were covered; (20) the waters swelled above the mountains, covering them fifteen cubits deep. (21) And all flesh died that moved on the earth, birds, domestic animals, wild animals, all swarming creatures that swarm on the earth, and all human beings; (22) everything on the dry land in whose nostrils was the breath of life died. (23) God blotted out every living thing that was on the face of the ground [ʾădāmāh], from human being [ʾādām] to beast to creeping thing to the birds of the air; they were blotted out from the earth. Only Noah was left, and those that were with him in the ark. (24) And the waters swelled on the earth for one hundred fifty days.

The narrator reports that events occurred as God had predicted: the flood continued until it was time to end, a period in which the ark floated on the rising waters. The waters were so deep that the highest point on the earth was buried under fifteen cubits. The extreme flooding left no air for the living creatures outside the ark to breathe, and they all died. The Hebrew does not distinguish between the ʾādām and other living creatures; all had need of air and, without air, all died. (In order to make the lack of distinction more evident in English, I have not used the NRSV but my own translation.) The text separates those in the ark—those with air and food, for whom God has provided the wherewithal to survive—from the others. The waters rained forty days but swelled for one hundred fifty. Whether verse 24 (150 days) represents a different source from verses 4, 12, and 17 (40 days), whether both numbers (150 and 40) are understood to represent completion, or whether the text asserts that the waters continued to rise after the rain stopped is unclear, and relatively unimportant for our purposes. The result remains the same, that just as the wood of the ark worked to save a segment of creation, water from the heavens and the deep worked to destroy the rest of creation.

> (8:1) But God remembered Noah and all the wild animals and all the domestic animals that were with him in the ark. And God made a wind blow over the earth, and the waters subsided; (2) the fountains of the deep and the windows of the heavens were closed, the rain from the heavens was restrained, (3) and the waters gradually receded from the earth. At the end of one hundred fifty days the waters had abated; (4) and in the seventh month, on the seventeenth day of the month, the ark came to rest on the mountains of Ararat. (5) The waters continued to abate until the tenth month; in the tenth month, on the first day of the month, the tops of the mountains appeared.

Like humankind, God remembers. Though the flood lasted forty days (or one hundred fifty days), it did end when appropriate. The waters ceased to come over the earth, and eventually began to recede. The rain had begun on the seventeenth day of the second month; it was not until the seventeenth day of the seventh month that the ark could rest on land. On the first day of the tenth month, the numbers again denoting completion, the tops of the mountains—land—were in sight.

> (8:6) At the end of forty days Noah opened the window of the ark that he had made (7) and sent out the raven; and it went to and fro until the waters were dried up from the earth. (8) Then he sent out the dove from him, to see if the waters had subsided from the face of the ground; (9) but the dove found no place to set its foot, and it returned to him to the ark, for the waters were still on the face of the whole earth. So he put out his hand and took it and brought it into the ark with him. (10) He waited another seven days, and again he sent out the dove from the ark; (11) and the dove came back to him in the evening, and there in its beak was a freshly plucked olive leaf; so Noah

knew that the waters had subsided from the earth. (12)
Then he waited another seven days, and sent out the dove;
and it did not return to him any more.

When the flood was over (after forty days, according to the
shortest time estimate), Noah sent forth a raven. The raven flew
until finding a dry place to perch. But the dove Noah sent next
returned without finding a perch, and, at the appropriate time
(after seven days, another measure of completion), Noah sent the
dove out again. Between the first and second flights much had
changed. The waters had receded to the point where life was acces-
sible. Noah waited before sending the dove out a third time, long
enough so the earth could support the bird. It no longer needed
the ark and did not return.

## Re-creation

### Genesis 8:13—9:7

> (8:13) In the six hundred first year, in the first month, the
> first day of the month, the waters were dried up from the
> earth; and Noah removed the covering of the ark, and
> looked, and saw that the face of the ground was drying. (14)
> In the second month, on the twenty-seventh day of the
> month, the earth was dry. (15) Then God said to Noah, (16)
> "Go out of the ark, you and your wife, and your sons and
> your sons' wives with you. (17) Bring out with you every liv-
> ing thing that is with you of all flesh—birds and animals
> and every creeping thing that creeps on the earth—so that
> they may abound on the earth, and be fruitful and multiply
> on the earth." (18) So Noah went out with his sons and his
> wife and his sons' wives. (19) And every animal, every
> creeping thing, and every bird, everything that moves on
> the earth, went out of the ark by families.

By the first day of the first month one year later, signifying a
new beginning, the ground was recovering from the flood. Almost
two months later, the Lord again gave direction to Noah regarding
himself, his family, and the other creatures with him; this time the

command was to "go out of the ark." At this new beginning, God directs that the creatures reproduce. The narrator reports that Noah's behavior is consistent with his earlier behavior: Noah obeys the Lord.

> (8:20) Then Noah built an altar to the LORD, and took of every clean animal and of every clean bird, and offered burnt offerings on the altar. (21) And when the LORD smelled the pleasing odor, the LORD said in his heart, "I will never again curse the ground because of humankind, for the inclination of the human heart is evil from youth; nor will I ever again destroy every living creature as I have done. (22) As long as the earth endures, seedtime and harvest, cold and heat, summer and winter, day and night, shall not cease."

Attributed to the Priestly source, these verses report that Noah offered some of the animals and birds from the seven pairs preserved as a sacrifice to God. The Lord's response to Noah's offering includes (1) a promise never again to destroy the ground (ʾădāmāh) because of humankind (ʾādām); (2) an assertion about ʾādām's propensity toward evil; (3) a promise never again to destroy all living things; and (4) a promise that nature's rhythms—planting and harvesting, temperatures and seasons—would continue as long as the earth existed.

> (9:1) God blessed Noah and his sons and said to them, "Be fruitful and multiply, and fill the earth."

The divine directive of reproduction offered in 8:17 to nonhuman animals surviving the flood is here expressly given to Noah and his family (cf. Gen. 1:28).

> (9:2) "The fear and dread of you shall rest on every animal of the earth, and on every bird of the air, on everything that creeps on the ground, and on all the fish of the sea; into your hand they are delivered. (3) Every moving thing that lives shall be food for you; and just as I gave you the green plants, I give you everything. (4) Only, you shall not eat flesh with its life, that is, its blood."

All nonhuman living creatures and all green plants are placed at the disposal of Noah's family—of humankind—for food. Humankind may consume everything except animals' blood. Gen. 9:2-4 is the first text explicitly to allow meat-eating among humankind, though such behavior may already have been implied.

> (9:5) "For your own lifeblood I will surely require a reckoning: from every animal I will require it and from human beings, each one for the blood of another, I will require a reckoning for human life. (6) Whoever sheds the blood of a human, by a human shall that person's life be shed; for in his own image God made humankind. (7) And you, be fruitful and multiply, abound on the earth and multiply in it."

No animal—human or nonhuman—may eat or shed human blood. The penalty for shedding the blood of one human being is the blood of another human being. The reason given for this prohibition is humankind's creation in the image of God; thus, divine protection of vulnerable humanity is secured (cf. Gen. 1:27).

This Genesis text, produced in a hierarchical culture, no doubt wishes to affirm humanity's value over the value of other creatures. Whereas humans may kill nonhuman animals for food, neither humans nor nonhuman animals may kill humans. Within ancient cultures, this prohibition may have functioned to inhibit cannibalism as well as murder.

## Covenant

### Genesis 9:8-19

> (8) Then God said to Noah and to his sons with him, (9) "As for me, I am establishing my covenant with you and your descendants after you, (10) and with every living creature that is with you, the birds, the domestic animals, and every animal of the earth with you, as many as came out of the ark. (11) I establish my covenant with you, that never again shall all flesh be cut off by the waters of a flood, and never

again shall there be a flood to destroy the earth." (12) God said, "This is the sign of the covenant that I make between me and you and every living creature that is with you, for all future generations: (13) I have set my bow in the clouds, and it shall be a sign of the covenant between me and the earth. (14) When I bring clouds over the earth and the bow is seen in the clouds, (15) I will remember my covenant that is between me and you and every living creature of all flesh; and the waters shall never again become a flood to destroy all flesh. (16) When the bow is in the clouds, I will see it and remember the everlasting covenant between God and every living creature of all flesh that is on the earth." (17) God said to Noah, "This is the sign of the covenant that I have established between me and all flesh that is on the earth."

God then establishes a relationship with the new creation, the representatives of whom are Noah and his family and all those other animals who were saved from the waters of the flood, such that God promises never again to destroy all flesh and the earth by a flood. As a sign of this promise, this covenant agreement, and as a reminder, God creates a rainbow in the clouds. Reiterated is the fact that this covenant is not made with Noah's family—humankind—only, but with "every living creature of all flesh on the earth."

(18) The sons of Noah who went out of the ark were Shem, Ham, and Japheth. Ham was the father of Canaan. (19) These three were the sons of Noah; and from these the whole earth was peopled.

The narrator reports that Noah's family obeyed the Lord's directive to leave the ark and to repopulate. One cannot help but notice that women are neither named nor credited with any role in reproduction, an obvious indicator of patriarchy. The reference to Ham's son Canaan serves as a transition to the narrative that follows.

# Thirsty Camels, Watering Sheep, and Brides
## Genesis 24:10-21

Just as water is essential to the survival of plants and to nonhuman and human animals, while at the same time existing as a potentially destructive force, the biblical text uses water also as a symbol for well-being and fertility. The woman who will become the bride of Sarah and Abraham's son Isaac is first introduced as working to procure water at a well. Her visit to the well, and her offer to procure water for Abraham's unnamed servant's thirsty camels, provides the occasion for identifying her as the daughter of Abraham's brother and as a fitting spouse for Isaac. Just as the humans of Rebekah's household depend on the water, so do Abraham's servant and the camels. An abundance of water, the life-securing element, foreshadows an abundance of well-being in the marriage.

> (10) Then the servant took ten of his master's camels and departed, taking all kinds of choice gifts from his master; and he set out and went to Aram-naharaim, to the city of Nahor. (11) He made the camels kneel down outside the city by the well of water; it was toward evening, the time when women go out to draw water. (12) And he said, "O Lord, God of my master Abraham, please grant me success today and show steadfast love to my master Abraham. (13) I am standing here by the spring of water, and the daughters of the townspeople are coming out to draw water. (14) Let the girl to whom I shall say, 'Please offer your jar that I may drink,' and who shall say, 'Drink, and I will water your camels'—let her be the one whom you have appointed for your servant Isaac. By this I shall know that you have shown steadfast love to my master."

The women did domestic chores, including drawing the water that was needed to quench their family's thirst and to wash. Apparently this task was better done, certainly more commonly done, after the heat of the day. If a woman consented to a stranger's request for water and also provided water for his animals—in this case ten thirsty camels—then she was the kind of person who would make a fit wife for the servant's master. The character analysis depends not on brains but on generosity; the number ten symbolizes completion, that is, provision for all of his animals. Abraham's servant hopes for a generous woman who will put herself out for the well-being of animals as well as for a stranger, an unnamed servant.

> (15) Before he had finished speaking, there was Rebekah, who was born to Bethuel son of Milcah, the wife of Nahor, Abraham's brother, coming out with her water jar on her shoulder. (16) The girl was very fair to look upon, a virgin, whom no man had known. She went down to the spring, filled her jar, and came up. (17) Then the servant ran to meet her and said, "Please let me sip a little water from your jar." (18) "Drink, my lord," she said, and quickly lowered her jar upon her hand and gave him a drink. (19) When she had finished giving him a drink, she said, "I will draw for your camels also, until they have finished drinking." (20) So she quickly emptied her jar into the trough and ran again to the well to draw, and she drew for all his camels. (21) The man gazed at her in silence to learn whether or not the LORD had made his journey successful.

Rebekah behaves just as Abraham's servant had hoped. She grants him a drink and adds, unsolicited, that she will also water his camels. She notes explicitly that she will water the camels until they have had their fill. The narrator informs the reader of the woman's name, and implicitly of her relationship to Abraham; but Abraham's servant still does not know who she is. Abraham was seeking, from his own kindred, a wife for his son, and his servant has found such a woman. The unnamed servant has also found a woman willing to share life-giving water with a human being who is a stranger, and with all his animals.

### Genesis 29:1-8

Just as the woman whom Isaac would marry was identified at a well, the woman Jacob would marry was similarly identified. Yet the circumstances differ. Whereas Abraham's servant identified Rebekah on Isaac's behalf, Jacob identifies Rachel for himself. In the narrative involving camels, Abraham's servant had possession of the animals, whereas in the Jacob narrative it is Rachel who has the sheep. The numbers ten and three signify completion in both stories. As Abraham's servant had ten camels, three flocks of sheep lie in the field near the well when Jacob comes upon it. Both women are described as working, but their work differs. Rebekah drew water; Rachel tends sheep. In both stories the watering of the animals is most appropriate in the evening, though it was already evening when Rebekah arrived to draw water, and it is not quite evening when Jacob arrives. As it is customary for the daughters of the townspeople to collect at the well in the evening to draw water, it is also customary for the shepherds to collect their flocks and then to remove the stone from the well mouth in order to water the sheep. Rachel's work with her father's sheep foreshadows Jacob's stay with her father and his difficulty in extricating his wives and sheep.

> (1) Then Jacob went on his journey, and came to the land of the people of the east. (2) As he looked, he saw a well in the field and three flocks of sheep lying there beside it; for out of that well the flocks were watered. The stone on the well's mouth was large, (3) and when all the flocks were gathered there, the shepherds would roll the stone from the mouth of the well, and water the sheep, and put the stone back in its place on the mouth of the well.

These verses set the scene, describing a fertile land with a well of life-sustaining water. The narrative informs us that three flocks of sheep are lying near the well in the field and that the sheep are accustomed to being watered, that is, having their thirst quenched, at the well. The well's water is protected from pollution—and people are protected from falling into the well—by a large stone that covers the well when the well is not in use.

> (4) Jacob said to them, "My brothers, where do you come from?" They said, "We are from Haran." (5) He said to them, "Do you know Laban son of Nahor?" They said, "We do." (6) He said to them, "Is it well with him?" "Yes," they replied, "and here is his daughter Rachel, coming with the sheep."

(7) He said, "Look, it is still broad daylight; it is not time for the animals to be gathered together. Water the sheep, and go, pasture them." (8) But they said, "We cannot until all the flocks are gathered together, and the stone is rolled from the mouth of the well; then we water the sheep."

The narrative indicates that Jacob knew that Rachel was the daughter of his mother's brother. He was seeking a bride from his family's kindred, and the woman coming with the sheep was such a person. Jacob seems to suggest that the shepherds should water their flocks (presumably the reason for their coming into the field where the well was), then leave the field to give them pasture for grazing. One could interpret Jacob's comment as a desire to be alone with Rachel; it seems more likely, though, that it was the sheep's well-being that he had in mind. Why cause sheep to lie in a field in broad daylight? It was much better for them (and for their owners) that they be allowed to graze. The shepherds' response to Jacob also seems attentive to the well-being of the sheep; the reason the sheep are waiting is that they cannot be watered until the other shepherds have arrived and rolled back the stone. The water is essential to the animals' well-being; it must be protected, hence, the stone. On the other hand, the sheep need to drink it, hence, the wait. The interdependence of all the characters in the narratives—the wells of water, the animals, and the human beings—should be particularly noted.

## Concern for the Weak

### Genesis 33:12-17

(12) Then Esau said, "Let us journey on our way, and I will go alongside you." (13) But Jacob said to him, "My lord knows that the children are frail and that the flocks and herds, which are nursing, are a care to me; and if they are overdriven for one day, all the flocks will die. (14) Let my lord pass on ahead of his servant, and I will lead on slowly, according to the pace of the cattle that are before me and according to the pace of the children, until I come to my lord in Seir."

(15) So Esau said, "Let me leave with you some of the people who are with me." But he said, "Why should my lord be so kind to me?" (16) So Esau returned that day on his way to Seir. (17) But Jacob journeyed to Succoth, and built himself a house, and made booths for his cattle; therefore the place is called Succoth.

This scene forms part of a larger unit recording the reconciliation of Esau and Jacob, which receives comment in the next section. In this text both brothers are depicted as concerned for the weak. Jacob, who had been concerned to establish himself as primary recipient of his father's blessing and as his father's heir—superior in status to his brother—expresses his concern for the vulnerable, for the frail children and the nursing flocks and herds. They—both humans and nonhumans—are in a physically vulnerable state and cannot be expected to travel at the pace of those who are stronger.

Jacob adjusts his behavior accordingly. He understands the risk of pushing the weak beyond the limits of their endurance, and chooses instead to let them set the pace of his journey. This description is a far cry from the man of power who coerces others to conform to his will, from the patriarch/hierarch who assumes that those less powerful should do his bidding and serve his pleasure. The text presents a man who lets the less powerful decide, lets the weaker chart the course, lets the animals make the decisions. Acknowledging this approach to his recently estranged brother Esau, he receives approbation, respect for his decision, and even an offer of help for the slower journey. Jacob responds to his brother with words of appreciation. There are no hints of superiority, only receptivity and mutuality.

While Esau can proceed directly to Seir, Jacob must stop along the way. He builds a house for protection from the elements for himself and implicitly for the frail children and for the others traveling with him; he then builds protection for the animals, "booths for his cattle."

## Reconciliation

### Genesis 32:3-21

Jacob and Esau were twin brothers; the younger, Jacob, supplanted the elder, Esau, first by buying his brother's birthright (Gen. 25:29-34) and then by deceiving his father Isaac to give him the blessing rightfully due his brother (Genesis 27). In order to prevent Esau from killing Jacob for what he had done, their mother Rebekah sent Jacob away, to her brother Laban's home in Haran. Years later, Jacob returns to his own land and his own people with fear and trepidation—not without cause.

> (3) Jacob sent messengers before him to his brother Esau in the land of Seir, the country of Edom, (4) instructing them, "Thus you shall say to my lord Esau: Thus says your servant Jacob, 'I have lived with Laban as an alien, and stayed until now; (5) and I have oxen, donkeys, flocks, male and female slaves; and I have sent to tell my lord, in order that I may find favor in your sight.'"

Jacob's strategy is to placate his brother with gifts. He first sends out a white flag in the form of messengers who announce Jacob's imminent arrival, but also just happen to mention Jacob's prosperity in the form of living possessions—servants and animals.

> (6) The messengers returned to Jacob, saying, "We came to your brother Esau, and he is coming to meet you, and four hundred men are with him." (7) Then Jacob was greatly afraid and distressed; and he divided the people that were with him, and the flocks and herds and camels, into two companies, (8) thinking, "If Esau comes to the one company and destroys it, then the company that is left will escape."
> (9) And Jacob said, "O God of my father Abraham and God of my father Isaac, O LORD who said to me, 'Return to your country and to your kindred, and I will do you good,' (10) I am not worthy of the least of all the steadfast love and all the faithfulness that you have shown to your servant, for with only my staff I crossed this Jordan; and now I have become two companies. (11) Deliver me, please, from the

hand of my brother, from the hand of Esau, for I am afraid of him; he may come and kill us all, the mothers with the children. (12) Yet you have said, 'I will surely do you good, and make your offspring as the sand of the sea, which cannot be counted because of their number.'"

When Jacob's messengers inform him that Esau is coming to meet him with four hundred men, Jacob is terrified, divides his possessions, and begins to pray.

> (13) So he spent the night there, and from what he had with him he took a present for his brother Esau, (14) two hundred female goats and twenty male goats, two hundred ewes and twenty rams, (15) thirty milch camels and their colts, forty cows and ten bulls, twenty female donkeys and ten male donkeys. (16) These he delivered into the hands of his servants, every drove by itself, and said to his servants, "Pass on ahead of me, and put a space between drove and drove." (17) He instructed the foremost, "When Esau my brother meets you, and asks you, 'To whom do you belong? Where are you going? And whose are these ahead of you?' (18) then you shall say, 'They belong to your servant Jacob; they are a present sent to my lord Esau; and moreover he is behind us.'" (19) He likewise instructed the second and the third and all who followed the droves, "You shall say the same thing to Esau when you meet him, (20) and you shall say, 'Moreover your servant Jacob is behind us.'" For he thought, "I may appease him with the present that goes ahead of me, and afterwards I shall see his face; perhaps he will accept me." (21) So the present passed on ahead of him. . . .

He then singles out specific possessions—goats, sheep, cattle, camels, and donkeys—which he intends to offer to Esau as appeasement. They are to precede him so that Esau will receive the gifts before he meets Jacob.

### Genesis 33:1-11

> (1) Now Jacob looked up and saw Esau coming, and four hundred men with him. So he divided the children among Leah and Rachel and the two maids. (2) He put the maids

with their children in front, then Leah with her children, and Rachel and Joseph last of all. (3) He himself went on ahead of them, bowing himself to the ground seven times, until he came near his brother.

Jacob's response to Esau's approach is to arrange his family, putting those closest to Jacob in affection farthest from Esau in distance. The action implies his fear/desperation and his desire to protect his loved ones. Jacob goes out to meet Esau, bowing seven times before him. Jacob seemingly is still filled with fear.

(4) But Esau ran to meet him, and embraced him, and fell on his neck and kissed him, and they wept. (5) When Esau looked up and saw the women and children, he said, "Who are these with you?" Jacob said, "The children whom God has graciously given your servant." (6) Then the maids drew near, they and their children, and bowed down; (7) Leah likewise and her children drew near and bowed down; and finally Joseph and Rachel drew near, and they bowed down.

Esau's response is disarming. He embraces Jacob. They weep. Jacob is no doubt overcome with emotion, all his fear turned to relief and gratitude. He had reason to expect battle because of what he had done to Esau and because of Esau's company. Instead he experiences an embrace of friendship, a welcome. To Esau's request that Jacob identify his multitude, Jacob presents his family. From those most distant—the maids and their children—to his most beloved Rachel and Joseph, each presents themselves to Esau.

(8) Esau said, "What do you mean by all this company that I met?" Jacob answered, "To find favor with my lord." (9) But Esau said, "I have enough, my brother; keep what you have for yourself." (10) Jacob said, "No, please; if I find favor with you, then accept my present from my hand; for truly to see your face is like seeing the face of God—since you have received me with such favor. (11) Please accept my gift that is brought to you, because God has dealt graciously with me, and because I have everything I want."

To Esau's question about the animals preceding Jacob, Jacob assures his brother that they are gifts intended for him. Esau rejects the gifts, asserting that he does not need them and that Jacob should keep them for himself. But Jacob, relieved beyond measure—this day his life as well as the lives of his wives, children, and servants have been spared—insists that Esau accept the gifts. Eventually Jacob convinces Esau to do so.

Animals function as a symbol; they are used, but they are valued. The humans in the narrative have come to depend for their livelihood and well-being on the animals named. It is important not to assume that the offer includes ten times more female animals than males because they are of lesser value. Rather, one male can impregnate ten females. Jacob's gift, which includes the gift's future potential, represents the fullness of fertility and is valuable indeed. Jacob understands the seriousness of his offense and knows it was not a trifling.

One might be tempted to assume a hierarchy at work when animals precede the humans in reaching Esau. A close reading, however, reveals that Jacob places himself before the women and children. Patriarchy would insist on Jacob's superior status and tend to extend him the maximum protection. Jacob's decision risks the possibility that the animals will be taken and that he will be killed, but that the women and children will be spared. At his birth Jacob confounded the expectations of patriarchy when he grasped Esau's heel (Gen. 25:26); here he acts counter to expectations by valuing the lives of the women and children more than his own.

Reconciliation is here made possible by forgiveness. Jacob does not receive what he deserves—punishment for his mistreatment of his brother; nor does Esau receive what he deserves. What *does* Esau deserve? Revenge? Payment? What is adequate payment? In this story, Esau accepts Jacob's offering to preserve Jacob's pride. Esau offers forgiveness and the possibility of reconciliation; Jacob offers the gifts to symbolize recognition of his offense and his desire to be reconciled. The symbol is accepted.

## Genesis 44:18—45:5

The reconciliation of Genesis 44:18—45:5 involves Jacob's sons, who were jealous of their father's special affection for their brother Joseph, the firstborn of Jacob's favored wife, Rachel. Having disposed of Joseph by selling him to Ishmaelite traders bound for Egypt, his brothers lead their father to believe that he is dead, devoured by a wild animal. It goes without saying that Joseph had reason to be angry with his brothers.

After Joseph's rise to power in Egypt, where he was distributing food during the famine, his half-brothers—including all of Jacob's sons but the youngest, the other son having been born to Rachel—come to Egypt to buy food. Joseph recognizes his brothers, though they do not recognize him. He might have anticipated their need to buy food and their consequent arrival, but they could not have anticipated that the second-in-command in Egypt, the one distributing food during the famine, was the brother they had sold into slavery.

The hearer/reader of the narrative is anxious about what will happen. Will Joseph order the execution of his brothers? The power balance has been reversed. The brothers who had physically dominated Joseph are now at the mercy of the leader who could dominate, even obliterate, them. He could, but would he?

Joseph delays the action and retards the resolution. He sells food to his brothers, but as a condition for their being able to buy more food he requires that they bring their youngest brother with them. When they eventually return with Benjamin, Joseph again sells them food. This time, however, he hides a silver cup in Benjamin's bag, and when it is found he orders that, as punishment for the alleged theft, Benjamin become his slave. Judah then pleads for his younger brother's return.

> (44:18) Judah stepped up to him [Joseph] and said, "O my lord, let your servant please speak a word in my lord's ears, and do not be angry with your servant; for you are like Pharaoh himself. (19) My lord asked his servants, saying, 'Have you a father or a brother?' (20) And we said to my lord, 'We have a father, an old man, and a young brother, the

child of his old age. His brother is dead; he alone is left of his mother's children, and his father loves him.' (21) Then you said to your servants, 'Bring him down to me so that I may set my eyes on him.' (22) We said to my lord, 'The boy cannot leave his father, for if he should leave his father, his father would die.' (23) Then you said to your servants, 'Unless your youngest brother comes down with you, you shall see my face no more.' (24) When we went back to your servant my father we told him the words of my lord. (25) And when our father said, 'Go again, buy us a little food,' (26) we said, 'We cannot go down. Only if our youngest brother goes with us, will we go down; for we cannot see the man's face unless our youngest brother is with us.' (27) Then your servant my father said to us, 'You know that my wife bore me two sons; (28) one left me, and I said, Surely he has been torn to pieces; and I have never seen him since. (29) If you take this one also from me, and harm comes to him, you will bring down my gray hairs in sorrow to Sheol.' (30) Now therefore, when I come to your servant my father and the boy is not with us, then, as his life is bound up in the boy's life, (31) when he sees that the boy is not with us, he will die; and your servants will bring down the gray hairs of your servant our father with sorrow to Sheol. (32) For your servant became surety for the boy to my father, saying, 'If I do not bring him back to you, then I will bear the blame in the sight of my father all my life.' (33) Now therefore, please let your servant remain as a slave to my lord in place of the boy; and let the boy go back with his brothers. For how can I go back to my father if the boy is not with me? I fear to see the suffering that would come upon my father."

Judah begs Joseph to allow him to remain in his brother's stead. The character of Judah has changed from one who had allowed one of his brothers, the most beloved of his father, to die. Now he is willing to accept slavery so that another brother, the one who now is the most beloved, can return. The reader does not know Judah's feelings about Benjamin. Perhaps they are no warmer than his feelings were for Joseph. What the reader does know, however, is that Judah's concern for his father has become great enough for him to choose servitude rather than to inflict another deep loss. He who wanted greater status, even to the point of eliminating perceived rivals, now chooses lesser status in the form of servitude.

> (45:1) Then Joseph could no longer control himself before all those who stood by him, and he cried out, "Send everyone away from me." So no one stayed with him when Joseph made himself known to his brothers. (2) And he wept so loudly that the Egyptians heard it, and the household of Pharaoh heard it. (3) Joseph said to his brothers, "I am Joseph. Is my father still alive?" But his brothers could not answer him, so dismayed were they at his presence.
>
> (4) Then Joseph said to his brothers, "Come closer to me." And they came closer. He said, "I am your brother, Joseph, whom you sold into Egypt. (5) And now do not be distressed, or angry with yourselves, because you sold me here; for God sent me here before you to preserve life."

Joseph is keenly affected by the change in his brother. When his brothers first came to Egypt, Joseph had teased them, aware that he who was once in their power now held over them a future of satisfaction or starvation. Yet Judah's change in attitude regarding power, expressed in his request to become Joseph's slave in Benjamin's stead, seems to have prompted a similar change in Joseph's attitude toward power. He could have punished his brothers—severely; he could have continued to hold power, of knowledge and of his identity, over them; he could have stipulated that the brothers bring their father to Egypt. Joseph, however, chose to level the playing field. He confessed to his brothers his identity. Though they at first were dismayed—with good reason—he disarms them. He assures them that whatever their intent in selling him to slavery, God had intended their behavior to produce good. And it had. The food Joseph provided saved many people and animals from starvation.

The narrative ends happily. The power of service replaces the power of domination. Jacob is reunited with his beloved Joseph, Rachel's firstborn son. Neither Judah nor Benjamin is enslaved.

Rather, Joseph forgives his brothers, they are reunited, and Jacob and his family receive food and fertile land in Goshen.

## Sleek Cows, Gaunt Cows
### Genesis 41:1-7, 15-36

(1) . . . Pharaoh dreamed that he was standing by the Nile, (2) and there came up out of the Nile seven sleek and fat cows, and they grazed in the reed grass. (3) Then seven other cows, ugly and thin, came up out of the Nile after them, and stood by the other cows on the bank of the Nile. (4) The ugly and thin cows ate up the seven sleek and fat cows. And Pharaoh awoke. (5) Then he fell asleep and dreamed a second time; seven ears of grain, plump and good, were growing on one stalk. (6) Then seven ears, thin and blighted by the east wind, sprouted after them. (7) The thin ears swallowed up the seven plump and full ears. Pharaoh awoke and it was a dream.

Pharaoh had two dreams representing the same idea. He first saw seven sleek and fat cows, which, even without a dream-interpreter, could be interpreted to represent prosperity; they fed on the reed grass along the banks of the Nile. Water, a symbol of fertility, and food for the animals complete the picture of well-being. Pharaoh then saw seven ugly and thin cows; though they also came up from the Nile, instead of eating the reed grass they proceeded to eat the seven sleek and fat cows. Their behavior is aberrant—cows eat grain, not other cows—and also represents the demise of the sleek and fat cows. The dream does not offer a happy picture, even if one does not understand its implications.

The second dream resembles the first, with ears of grain replacing the cows. Pharaoh first sees seven ears of plump and good grain growing on one stalk. Again, a full stalk could be interpreted to represent prosperity. Pharaoh then saw another stalk sprouting, this stalk containing seven thin and ugly ears blighted by the east wind. Rather than providing a source of food for other living things, the thin ears devoured the existing food, the plump and good ears of grain. Again, the sight is not pleasant.

(15) And Pharaoh said to Joseph, "I have had a dream, and there is no one who can interpret it. I have heard it said of you that when you hear a dream you can interpret it." (16) Joseph answered Pharaoh, "It is not I; God will give Pharaoh a favorable answer." (17) Then Pharaoh said to Joseph, "In my dream I was standing on the banks of the Nile; (18) and seven cows, fat and sleek, came up out of the Nile and fed in the reed grass. (19) Then seven other cows came up after them, poor, very ugly, and thin. Never had I seen such ugly ones in all the land of Egypt. (20) The thin and ugly cows ate up the first seven fat cows, (21) but when they had eaten them no one would have known that they had done so, for they were still as ugly as before. Then I awoke. (22) I fell asleep a second time and I saw in my dream seven ears of grain, full and good, growing on one stalk, (23) and seven ears, withered, thin, and blighted by the east wind, sprouting after them; (24) and the thin ears swallowed up the seven good ears. . . .

(25) Then Joseph said to Pharaoh, "Pharaoh's dreams are one and the same; God has revealed to Pharaoh what he is about to do. (26) The seven good cows are seven years, and the seven good ears are seven years; the dreams are one. (27) The seven lean and ugly cows that came up after them are seven years, as are the seven empty ears blighted by the east wind. They are seven years of famine. . . . (29) There will come seven years of great plenty throughout all the land of Egypt. (30) After them there will arise seven years of famine, and all the plenty will be forgotten in the land of Egypt; the famine will consume the land. (31) The plenty will no longer be known in the land because of the famine that will follow, for it will be very grievous. (32) And the doubling of Pharaoh's dream means that the thing is fixed by God, and God will shortly bring it about."

The dreams together form one dream. All the sources of food—reed grass, ears of grain, sleek and fat cows—have been devoured or destroyed. Since seven can refer symbolically to completion, the loss of seven cows and seven ears of grain means that nothing is left.

Pharaoh seeks out an interpreter for his dreams and eventually discovers Joseph, who says that God is telling Pharaoh what the future holds: seven prosperous years will precede seven years of famine.

The term *famine* does not fall on our ears with the same weight as it would have with our ancestors. Nor can we in the First World fully grasp what a seven-year famine could effect. Virtually nothing would survive—no grain to feed the animals, no grain and animals to feed human beings. A seven-year famine delivers the impact of a forty-day flood. What living thing(s) can survive?

> (33) "Now therefore let Pharaoh select a man who is discerning and wise, and set him over the land of Egypt. (34) Let Pharaoh proceed to appoint overseers over the land, and take one-fifth of the produce of the land of Egypt during the seven plenteous years. (35) Let them gather all the food of these good years that are coming, and lay up grain under the authority of Pharaoh for food in the cities, and let them keep it. (36) That food shall be a reserve for the land against the seven years of famine that are to befall the land of Egypt, so that the land may not perish through the famine."

Joseph goes beyond the dream's interpretation. Since God has shown Pharaoh the future, Joseph suggests a way, not to change the future, but to prepare and to prevent total destruction. Just as Noah was provided with an ark lest everything be destroyed (Genesis 6–9), God provides Pharaoh with foreknowledge so provisions can be saved for the years of famine. Joseph, the former prisoner who interpreted Pharaoh's dreams, becomes the "discerning and wise" man who would ensure the land's endurance through the famine.

## Sharing Resources and Preserving Life
### Genesis 42:25; 44:1; 45:5-7

These verses are buried in the Joseph narrative and might easily be lost. It is important to note their depiction of Joseph in a clear position of power, controlling the food supply on which his brothers depend. Although their earlier treatment of him might have prompted Joseph to reject their request for food, he does not.

> (42:25) Joseph then gave orders to fill their [his brothers'] bags with grain, to return every man's money to his sack, and to give them provisions for their journey. This was done for them.

Joseph's brothers have come to Egypt to buy grain. A fair response would be grain in exchange for payment, but Joseph does not respond as the reader might expect. Rather, he fulfills their request—he gives them the grain—but he also returns their money to them. Further, he adds provisions for their journey home.

> (44:1) Then he [Joseph] commanded the steward of his house, "Fill the men's sacks with food, as much as they can carry, and put each man's money in the top of his sack."

Joseph is in a position of plenty as the distributor of the food his brothers desperately need. With his response he does not try to enhance his power, to take advantage of a limited supply and maximum demand; rather, he gives from his abundance of grain and food. He is in a position to share, and does.

> (45:5) "And now, do not be distressed, or angry with yourselves, because you sold me here; for God sent me before you to preserve life. (6) For the famine has been in the land these two years; and there are five more years in which there will be neither plowing nor harvest. (7) God sent me before you to preserve for you a remnant on earth, and to keep alive for you many survivors."

Joseph's self-understanding comes in relationship—not only to his brothers but to his God. It is God who, according to Joseph, has sent him to Egypt. While his brothers' motives may have been contrary to Joseph's best interests, God showed interest not only in Joseph's good but in the good of many. Joseph understands himself as God's instrument "to preserve life," that is, to provide to the

Egyptians and surrounding peoples and to their animals. The interdependence of Joseph's brothers, Joseph, God, servants, and animals is evident throughout. Sharing resources preserves life.

## Provision for All

### Exodus 23:10-12

> (10) For six years you shall sow your land and gather in its yield; (11) but the seventh year you shall let it rest and lie fallow, so that the poor of your people may eat; and what they leave the wild animals may eat. You shall do the same with your vineyard, and with your olive orchard.
>
> (12) Six days you shall do your work, but on the seventh day you shall rest, so that your ox and your donkey may have relief, and your homeborn slave and the resident alien may be refreshed.

The Priestly account of creation (Gen. 1:1—2:4a) provides for six days of work and, on the seventh day, a period for God's rest. God has established a rhythm of work and rest. In the Exodus text, another reason for the sabbath becomes clear: so that others may benefit.

With regard to the land, in the year it is not cultivated the poor may gather what the land produces. The poor usually could glean what reapers had left; in this case, however, there would be no reapers, and the poor could take whatever the land produced. The writer assumes such an abundance of produce that leftovers will remain for the wild animals. Leaving the land fallow for a year restores nutrients so, in fact, everyone benefits, even persons who normally sow.

The law provides similarly for vineyards and olive orchards. Instead of cultivating the vines and taking the grapes and olives, owners are to give the vines a rest. The provision guarantees grapes and olives for the poor and the animals. Again, such behavior benefits the vineyards and the orchards and, consequently, their owners as well.

Finally, everyone is to rest on the seventh day—not only the land and the vineyards and the orchards, but the people as well. This rest is especially important for giving relief to the ox and the donkey from the loads they ordinarily must pull or carry. It is also important for slaves and aliens, those who do not own the land but who work on it. If they are to be refreshed after their physical labor, they need rest. It is to the benefit of everyone—to vulnerable humans, especially the poor, the children of servants, and resident aliens, and animals (wild and domesticated)—and everything (agricultural lands, vineyards, and orchards) that all should have rest.

## Blessings

### Leviticus 26:3-13

> (3) If you follow my statutes and keep my commandments and observe them faithfully, (4) I will give you your rains in their season, and the land shall yield its produce, and the trees of the field shall yield their fruit.

Other Pentateuchal texts cite God's promises of blessing to the people if they are faithful (e.g., Deut. 28:1-14). This text highlights that on which human beings depend, that which they understand God as providing. If God supplies rain during the rainy season, the prospect is good for an abundant harvest from both the plants (vegetables) in the fields and the fruit in the trees.

> (5) Your threshing shall overtake the vintage, and the vintage shall overtake the sowing; you shall eat your bread to the full, and live securely in your land.

The abundance that God promises is so plentiful that the farmers' efforts will lag behind what nature produces. Grapes will be waiting to be threshed; new seed, before being sown, will await the harvesting of what has already been planted. There will be no scarcity of food.

> (6) And I will grant peace in the land, and you shall lie down, and no one shall make you afraid; I will remove dangerous animals from the land, and no sword shall go through your land. (7) You shall give chase to your enemies, and they shall fall before you by the sword. (8) Five of you

shall give chase to a hundred, and a hundred of you shall give chase to ten thousand; your enemies shall fall before you by the sword.

In order to live securely, any people must have an adequate food supply. But there are other needs also. Their land need be free from fear-inducing, lift-threatening dangers. Vicious and voracious animals such as lions and wolves, preying on land, animals, and people, could present one danger. Yet God promises that the dangerous animals will be removed. Another danger could be in the form of invading armies. God promises the Israelites that attacking warriors will not be able to penetrate. The Israelites, in defending themselves and the land, will pursue those bearing swords against them and will triumph. Only a few Israelites will be needed to secure victory against potential invaders large in number. With God on their side, the victory is not only secure; it is overwhelming. God promises and provides peace in the land.

> (9) I will look with favor upon you and make you fruitful and multiply you; and I will maintain my covenant with you. (10) You shall eat old grain long stored, and you shall have to clear out the old to make way for the new.

Reiterating God's promise to provide sufficient food is the implication that excess food ("old grain") will have been placed in abundance in storehouses. People will have to clear out the excess to make way for the excess of new grain.

To sufficient—even abundant—food, and victory over animal and human threat, God adds the blessing of fertility. The people themselves will multiply.

> (11) I will place my dwelling in your midst, and I shall not abhor you. (12) And I will walk among you, and will be your God, and you shall be my people. (13) I am the LORD your God who brought you out of the land of Egypt, to be their slaves no more; I have broken the bars of your yoke and made you walk erect.

The Lord asserts a continuation of his covenant relationship with the people. God will be in their midst, looking favorably toward them. Walking among them—*walking* is a formal covenant term—the Lord promises to be the Israelites' god with the Israelites as the Lord's people. The God of the Israelites, the God whose statutes the Israelites are called to obey, is the One who redeemed the people from Egyptian bondage, the One who set them free.

## Neighborliness
### Deuteronomy 22:1-4, 6-8

> (1) You shall not watch your neighbor's ox or sheep straying away and ignore them; you shall take them back to their owner. (2) If the owner does not reside near you or you do not know who the owner is, you shall bring it to your own house, and it shall remain with you until the owner claims it; then you shall return it. (3) You shall do the same with a neighbor's donkey; you shall do the same with a neighbor's garment; and you shall do the same with anything else that your neighbor loses and you find. You may not withhold your help.
>
> (4) You shall not see you neighbor's donkey or ox fallen on the road and ignore it; you shall help to lift it up.

The laws enumerated here imply that one has responsibility for the well-being of others in one's community. Clearly and unequivocally, if another person's animals—or any possession for that matter—escapes or becomes lost, one has an obligation to return the straying animal or lost object to its owner, or at least to stand ready to return lost possessions when claimed. One cannot remain indifferent to ill that occurs to another's possessions; rather, one must actively intervene to restore the other's possessions and, by implication, the other's well-being. This is certainly true in the case of human beings.

(6) If you come on a bird's nest, in any tree or on the ground, with fledglings or eggs, with the mother sitting on the fledglings or on the eggs, you shall not take the mother with the young. (7) Let the mother go, taking only the young for yourself, in order that it may go well with you and you may live long.

When a bird is concerned, in this case, a bird with young or potential young, one is instructed not to be greedy. Although one may take the young, one is instructed to let the mother go. One's own well-being depends on how one treats the birds.

(8) When you build a new house, you shall make a parapet for your roof; otherwise you might have bloodguilt on your house, if anyone should fall from it.

Finally, one must protect others from potential harm. With regard to the roof one provides for a house under construction, it must be built with a parapet in order to prevent someone from falling off the edge.

The laws cited above imply that individuals have rights to keep someone else's property if the person lives far away or is a stranger, to take the young of a mother bird, and to build a house. But individuals also have obligations to behave proactively and to prevent another person's animals from straying, to return the property of a person who lives nearby and is known, to release a mother bird, and to build a parapet as part of one's roof. These obligations or responsibilities derive from the author's consciousness that people live interdependently with other people and with other living creatures.

# 2

# Use, Not Abuse

## An Ark for Protection

### *Genesis 6:11-22*

> (11) Now the earth was corrupt in God's sight, and the earth was filled with violence. (12) And God saw that the earth was corrupt; for all flesh had corrupted its ways upon the earth. (13) And God said to Noah, "I have determined to make an end of all flesh, for the earth is filled with violence because of them; now I am going to destroy them along with the earth."

A close reading reveals that "the earth was corrupt in God's sight," not merely human beings. The corruption is related to violence, or at least violence reinforces God's assertion that the earth is corrupt. Because of the violence on the earth, a violence perpetrated, again, not just by human beings but by "all flesh," including other animals, God asserts the intention of destroying the whole project of creation, the earth which God has created and the living beings who dwell therein.

> (14) "Make yourself an ark of cypress wood; make rooms in the ark, and cover it inside and out with pitch. (15) This is how you are to make it: the length of the ark three hundred cubits, its width fifty cubits, and its height thirty cubits. (16)

Make a roof for the ark, and finish it to a cubit above; and put the door of the ark in its side; make it with lower, second, and third decks."

But after declaring the intent to destroy, God commands Noah to build. God commands creative activities, not destructive ones. Noah is to build the ark from cypress wood, from cypress trees, which will be at the service of Noah's well-being, his physical survival.

(17) "For my part, I am going to bring a flood of waters on the earth, to destroy from under heaven all flesh in which is the breath of life; everything that is on the earth shall die.

God states that the earth will be destroyed by flood. The water will destroy all living, breathing beings.

(18) But I will establish my covenant with you; and you shall come into the ark, you, your sons, your wife, and your sons' wives with you. (19) And of every living thing, of all flesh, you shall bring two of every kind into the ark, to keep them alive with you; they shall be male and female. (20) Of the birds according to their kinds, and of the animals according to their kinds, of every creeping thing of the ground according to its kind, two of every kind shall come in to you, to keep them alive. (21) Also take with you every kind of food that is eaten, and store it up; and it shall serve as food for you and for them." (22) Noah did this; he did all that God commanded him.

Verse 18 is critical to the narrative. Is this story about a flood, an ark, or a covenant? Of what does the covenant consist? Who are parties to the covenant? Who benefits?

God tells Noah that he himself is to go into the ark, the narrative implying that the ark God has instructed Noah to build will protect him from the floodwaters. But an ark is not enough to protect Noah. For him to survive, he needs food and other people. Thus God directs Noah to bring his family into the ark—his wife, his sons, and their wives. Noah's future, represented by his family, is protected by the ark. Historians believe that the people who produced this text did not believe in life after death; therefore, if Noah were to live after his death, it could only be through his descendants.

God instructs Noah to bring into the ark two of all flesh—male and female, with the potential for fertility. The very flesh that had committed violence and was to be destroyed would also, through a remnant, be preserved. Birds, animals, creeping creatures—each would have representative survivors. In order that all these living beings might eat, God instructed Noah to bring every kind of food, and excess food for storage, onto the ark. Though the text does not mention plants explicitly, we may conclude that the "flesh" preserved on the ark consumed plants for food.

The narrator comments that Noah, elsewhere described as righteous, blameless, and walking with God, becomes God's covenant partner. Noah does everything that God tells him to do; because he does, a remnant of all creation is saved.

## Animals for Food
### Genesis 9: 2-3

> (2) The fear and dread of you shall rest on every animal of the earth, and on every bird of the air, on everything that creeps on the ground, and on all the fish of the sea; into your hand they are delivered. (3) Every moving thing that lives shall be food for you; and just as I gave you the green plants, I give you everything.

Until this point in the Genesis narrative, of food provided for human beings, explicit mention has been made only of plants. In Gen. 1:29 God tells the man and woman that every plant yielding seed and every tree with seed in its fruit shall be theirs. Though they are given "dominion over the fish of the sea, and over the birds of the air . . . and over every creeping thing that creeps upon the earth" (1:26), no explicit mention is made of humankind's right to eat flesh. In Gen. 2:16-17 God tells the 'ādām that he may eat freely of every tree in the garden except the tree of the knowledge of good and evil. After the man eats from the forbidden tree (Gen. 3:17-19), a curse promises difficulty in taking food from the ground: "Cursed is the ground because of you; in toil you shall eat of it all the days of your life; thorns and thistles it shall bring forth for you; and you shall eat the plants of the field. By the sweat of your face you shall eat bread. . . ."

Now, after the destruction caused by the flood, a re-creation takes place. As the woman and man of Gen. 1:28 are told to "be fruitful and multiply, and [to] fill the earth and subdue it," God tells the human survivors of the flood to "be fruitful and multiply, and fill the earth" (9:1). To the plants that they had initially been given as food are added all the animals. Whereas the narrative previously had allowed them to subdue and have dominion over birds, fish, and the animals, they now are told that all the animals are also at their disposal as food.

When one thinks about harvest and plant preservation, one realizes that a diet composed solely of plant food might not have been sufficient. One need only note the number of times biblical texts refer to "famine in the land" (e.g., Gen. 12:10, 26:1, and throughout chaps. 41–47). Eating the flesh of birds, fish, and animals killed for that purpose would be essential for survival.

But the animals are not stupid. Once birds, creeping creatures, fish, and other animals realize that human beings seek to kill them, they will be in "fear and dread" of human beings; to the extent they are able, they will flee.

## Bread, Clothing, and Water
### Genesis 28:20-22

Gen. 28:20-22 follows a dream of Jacob, which occurs en route to Haran to secure a wife from his mother's family. God appeared to him in the dream, identified as the God of his father Abraham and Isaac, and promised to grant Jacob the land on which he stood and offspring like the "dust of the earth" (28:14). God promises to stay with Jacob and to keep him safe until his return. Verses 20-22 represent Jacob's response to God's presence and God's promise.

(20) Then Jacob made a vow, saying, "If God will be with me, and will keep me in this way that I go, and will give me bread to eat and clothing to wear, (21) so that I come again to my father's house in peace, then the LORD shall be my God, and this stone, which I have set up for a pillar, shall be God's house; and of all that you give me I will surely give one tenth to you."

If God is faithful to the promise, that is, if God provides Jacob with divine presence, guidance, and protection, then the stone on which Jacob's head had lain will be set aside as God's house. Specifying particulars of God's guidance and protection, Jacob states that to return safely he will need food, that is "bread," and clothing, recognizing these items as essential elements of God's provision for well-being. If God fulfills the promise, Jacob pledges to return one-tenth of God's gifts to God.

The literary unit is covenantal. God's self-revelation is as the God of Jacob's ancestors; God is and will be Jacob's god. That is the promise which Jacob accepts. He depends on his God for survival and well-being; he knows, and explicitly asserts, that his survival depends on food and clothing.

### Deuteronomy 2:6-7

At the beginning of Moses' farewell speech in Deuteronomy, Moses recalls events demonstrating God's care for his people during the desert journey. He recalls God's words to him regarding the people's passage through the land of Seir, belonging to Esau's descendants, when the Israelites were commanded not to engage in battle. God had given that land to the descendants of Esau, it was explained, and would not give it to the Israelites.

(6) You shall purchase food from them for money, so that you may eat; and you shall also buy water from them for money, so that you may drink. (7) Surely the LORD your God has blessed you in all your undertakings; he knows your going through this great wilderness. These forty years the LORD your God has been with you; you have lacked nothing.

During the time it would take for the Israelites to pass through the land, they would need food and water to survive. God commanded Moses to buy these necessities from the people whose land they traversed. Since God knew they needed these items, the Israelites had every reason to expect that God would make it possible for the Israelites to procure them. But, God told Moses, they must procure the items for money, in honest exchange, and not by violence and conquest. The text implies that one cannot just take what belongs to another—in this case, even food and water.

### Deuteronomy 8:3-4

Continuing his reminiscences about the Israelites' time in the desert, Moses recalls the Israelites' complaints and the opportunities God provided them to deepen their relationship with God and to understand more fully their dependence. Hunger represented one such opportunity.

> (3) He [God] humbled you by letting you hunger, then by feeding you with manna, with which neither you nor your ancestors were acquainted, in order to make you understand that one does not live by bread alone, but by every word that comes from the mouth of the Lord. (4) The clothes on your back did not wear out and your feet did not swell these forty years.

Without food the Israelites would die; but God could, and did, provide it. Their survival depended not so much on food, per se, but on God. God would provide for their needs, and God did provide for their needs. In addition to the manna, God ensured that their clothes would last, lest their health diminish and they die of exposure, and that their feet would not swell, lest they be unable to travel to the land God had promised. The physical needs of humans—in this case, of the Israelites—are real, and include food; but the text assures its readers that human beings are dependent on God to meet these needs.

*Deuteronomy 29:5-6*

Toward the end of Moses' farewell speech, he reiterates how God has provided for the Israelites during forty years in the desert, how God has brought them to their present site overlooking the land God has promised, and how God has met their physical needs during all their wanderings.

> (5) I have led you forty years in the wilderness. The clothes on your back have not worn out, and the sandals on your feet have not worn out; (6) you have not eaten bread, and you have not drunk wine or strong drink—so that you may know that I am the LORD your God.

For the Israelites to have survived, God had to provide food—not bread but manna; this food was not their achievement, but God's. God provided drink—not wine but water; this water was not their achievement, but God's. The Israelites, strangely enough, did not have to replace worn clothing, for God made sure their clothing endured. Nor did they lack sandals, since, despite the travel, their sandals did not wear out. Moses tells the people that these things happened so that they would know their God. The God who is God of these human beings is also the God of all creation, the God who can meet the needs of the people and provide them food, water, sandals, and other clothing.

## Trees

*Leviticus 19:23-25*

> (23) When you come into the land and plant all kinds of trees for food, then you shall regard their fruit as forbidden; three years it shall be forbidden to you, it must not be eaten. (24) In the fourth year all their fruit shall be set apart for rejoicing in the LORD. (25) But in the fifth year you may eat of their fruit, that their yield may be increased for you: I am the LORD your God.

If fruit trees are to yield abundant fruit, according to Lev. 19:23-25, they must be allowed to take root over time. Usually the first years after they have been planted they simply do not produce fruit, or the fruit they produce is not worth eating, that is, not of adequate size and quality. The law provides respect for the fruit tree, allowance for its development according to its own time and particular gene properties, and a stricture that it not be raped before harvest. This provision of law does not allow human beings to abuse nature for their ends, but allows human beings to use nature, after waiting patiently until nature provides, and then to respond with joy and gratitude for nature's bounty.

### Deuteronomy 20:19-20

> (19) If you besiege a town for a long time, making war against it in order to take it, you must not destroy its trees by wielding an ax against them. Although you may take food from them, you must not cut them down. Are trees in the field human beings that they should come under siege from you? (20) You may destroy only the trees that you know do not produce food; you may cut them down for use in building siegeworks against the town that makes war with you, until it falls.

Deut. 20:19 distinguishes between the violence of warfare and the violence of using an ax to cut down trees. While engaged in warfare, one may not extend that violence to trees. Although twentieth-century readers might assume that human beings are more valuable than trees, and, therefore, warfare a more serious activity than tree-cutting, the text is clear: one act of violence does not justify the other. While it is appropriate to take fruit from trees, it is wrong to destroy fruit-bearing trees. The inappropriateness of tree-cutting for building siegeworks is highlighted by the question, "Are trees in the field human beings that they should come under siege from you?"

Deut. 20:20 particularizes the preceding verse by differentiating between fruit-bearing trees and other trees. While the fruit of food-bearing trees may be eaten, and thus provide sustenance to human beings, the tree itself may not be destroyed to build siegeworks against one's enemy. The reader is called to appreciate what fruit trees provide and to appreciate and nurture them, not to destroy them. The text asserts, however, that trees that do not produce food can be used in siegeworks. The text calls one to respect the differences between trees and to recognize the particular contribution each has made to the well-being of humankind.

## Able, God-Fearing Men to Judge the People

### Exodus 18:13-26

(13) The next day Moses sat as judge for the people, while the people stood around him from morning until evening. (14) When Moses' father-in-law saw all that he was doing for the people, he said, "What is this that you are doing for the people? Why do you sit alone, while all the people stand around you from morning until evening?"

(15) Moses said to his father-in-law, "Because the people come to me to inquire of God. (16) When they have a dispute, they come to me and I decide between one person and another, and I make known to them the statutes and instructions of God."

Exod. 18:13 portrays Moses as judge for/over the Israelites, who come to him when they wish to inquire of God. They come with disputes, explain the circumstances, and allow him to make some judgment—to side with one of the disputants. The implication is that Moses will inquire of God on their behalf. Moses also functions as judge when he makes known the statutes and instructions of God. These activities, as Moses' father-in-law observed, take all of Moses' time, "from morning until evening."

(17) Moses' father-in law said to him, "What you are doing is not good. (18) You will surely wear yourself out, both you and these people with you. For the task is too heavy for you; you cannot do it alone. (19) Now listen to me. I will give you counsel, and God be with you! You should represent the people before God, and you should bring their cases before God; (20) teach them the statutes and instructions and make known to them the way they are to go and the things they are to do."

Moses' father-in-law advises Moses that his task as judge is too much for one person. He counsels Moses to represent the people before God, to bring their cases before God, and to teach them God's statutes and instructions. Moses had been doing these tasks all along, but he had been doing them by himself.

> (21) "You should also look for able men among all the people, men who fear God, are trustworthy, and hate dishonest gain; set such men over them as officers over thousands, hundreds, fifties, and tens. (22) Let them sit as judges for the people at all times; let them bring every important case to you, but decide every minor case themselves. So it will be easier for you, and they will bear the burden with you. (23) If you do this, and God so commands you, then you will be able to endure, and all these people will go to their home in peace."

The second part of Moses' father-in-law's advice—to enlist others in performing his tasks as judge—required that these men deal with the minor cases. They, like Moses, would bring the people's cases before God, but would deal with the less important matters.

The advice restricts judgeships to those who were able *('anšê-ḥayil)*, who feared God, who were trustworthy *('anšê-'emet)*, and who hated dishonest gain. The plan would help Moses endure the weight of the work, and the people would get a fair hearing.

> (24) So Moses listened to his father-in-law and did all that he had said. (25) Moses chose able men from all Israel and appointed them as heads over the people, as officers over thousands, hundreds, fifties, and tens. (26) And they judged the people at all times; hard cases they brought to Moses, but any minor case they decided themselves.

Moses was smart and humble enough to take his father-in-law's advice and to accept help from other worthy men. The organizational structure, with officers appointed over groups of ten, fifty, one hundred, and a thousand, was meant to give access to leadership to all people. The requirement of integrity and the delineation of the judges' tasks and power was meant to prevent abuse.

Though men are envisioned in this organizational structure, Miriam, Moses' sister, clearly emerges as a leader. She is identified not as a *šōpēt*, a judge, but as a *nĕbî'āh*, a prophet (Exod. 15:20).

### Deuteronomy 1:9-17

> (9) At that time I said to you, "I am unable by myself to bear you. (10) The LORD your God has multiplied you, so that today you are as numerous as the stars of heaven. (11) May the LORD, the God of your ancestors, increase you a thousand times more and bless you, as he has promised you! (12) But how can I bear the heavy burden of your disputes all by myself? (13) Choose for each of your tribes individuals who are wise, discerning, and reputable to be your leaders."
>
> (14) You answered me, "The plan you have proposed is a good one."

Within the summary of Israel's history contained in Moses' farewell speech in Deuteronomy, we read another version of the appointment of judges. In this account it is not Moses' father-in-law who observes the enormity of Moses' work, but Moses himself who realizes that the ever increasing number of Israelites is affecting his workload. While rejoicing in Israel's population increase and wishing for its continued fecundity, he realizes that settling the disputes among them is becoming too much. He therefore suggests that the people choose men who are "wise, discerning, and reputable" to function as leaders. The people support his proposal.

> (15) So I took the leaders of your tribes, wise and reputable individuals, and installed them as leaders over you, commanders of thousands, commanders of hundreds, commanders of fifties, commanders of tens, and officials, throughout your tribes. (16) I charged your judges at that time: "Give the members of your community a fair hearing, and judge rightly between one person and another, whether citizen or resident alien. (17) You must not be partial in judging: hear out the small and the great alike; you shall not be intimidated by anyone, for the judgment is God's. Any case that is too hard for you, bring to me, and I will hear it."

Moses determines the tasks of the judges: to give people a fair hearing; to judge rightly between persons regardless of their status as citizens or resident aliens; to be impartial in judging between small and great; and to avoid being intimidated. All cases too difficult for the installed judges were to be referred to Moses.

In contrast to Exodus 18:13-26 above, this passage gives explicit reminder that the judgment is God's. Moses and the judges function on God's behalf. It should be added that a woman, Deborah, is identified as a judge in Judges 4–5. Like Miriam (see also Exod. 15:20), Deborah, the wife of Lappidoth, is described as a prophetess: "She used to sit under the palm of Deborah . . . and the Israelites came up to her for judgment" (Judg. 4:5). The narrative clearly depicts her as possessing the qualities appropriate to Israel's judges. She was not easily intimidated and was "wise, discerning, and reputable" (Deut. 1:13).

# 3

# The Land: A Promised Treasure

## Sacred Land between Bethel and Ai

*Genesis 12:7*

> Then the LORD appeared to Abram, and said, "To your off-spring I will give this land." So he built there an altar to the LORD, who had appeared to him.

This text is one of many in the Pentateuch that stakes out sacred land because of what takes place there. The place described is made sacred by the appearance and promise of God, and by the altar to God that Abram builds; thus it is holy. In Gen. 12:1 God instructs Abram to go to the place God will show him. Abram obeys: "When [Abram and company] had come to the land of Canaan, Abram passed through the land to the place at Shechem, to the oak of Moreh. At that time the Canaanites were in the land" (vv. 5-6).

Verse 7 contains the first declaration of God's promise to Abram to provide a land for his offspring. In order to become a people and to fulfill God's promise to Abram in verse 2, one must have land. In the ancient Near East no people could survive without land, the provider of water, food, and protection from enemies.

## Sacred Land at Mamre
### Genesis 13:14-17

(14) The LORD said to Abram, after Lot had separated from him, "Raise your eyes now, and look from the place where you are, northward and southward and eastward and westward; (15) for all the land that you see I will give to you and to your offspring forever. (16) I will make your offspring like the dust of the earth; so that if one can count the dust of the earth, your offspring also can be counted. (17) Rise up, walk through the length and the breadth of the land, for I will give it to you."

The Bible contains several promises of land to the patriarchs and matriarchs of ancient Israel. This passage emphasizes the extent of the land and connects its size to the number of people, Abram's offspring, who will populate it. Lot had separated from Abram because their respective flocks and herds as well as their families had increased so that the land on which they were dwelling together could no longer support them (vv. 5-6). Similarly, the text predicts that Abram's family would increase so that its boundaries would stretch "northward and southward and eastward and westward," that is, to *every place,* as far as the eye can see. Abram's offspring would be like the "dust of the earth," that is, *innumerable.* The intent of the promise as well as its expected effect was one of limitlessness. Yet, lest the promise remain abstract and beyond comprehension, the Lord instructs Abram to travel through the land. The land is real and concrete and to be fully experienced, a gift of God.

## Covenanted Land
### Genesis 15:18-21

(18) On that day the LORD made a covenant with Abram, saying, "To your descendants I give this land, from the river of Egypt to the great river, the river Euphrates, (19) the land of the Kenites, the Kenizzites, the Kadmonites, (20) the Hittites, the Perizzites, the Rephaim, (21) the Amorites, the Canaanites, the Girgashites, and the Jebusites."

The Bible asserts God's promise to Abram of land in several passages, including Gen. 12:7 and 13:14-17, and in this text the narrator formalizes the promise, calling it a covenant. The land described is extensive, stretching from the Nile to the Euphrates. The description could be a concrete reference to all the land between those bodies of water, or perhaps the reference is limited to the land between the rivers occupied by the ten named ethnic groups. The verse may merely imply that the Israelites will have a large land, relatively speaking, and be numerous. But since ten often symbolizes completion, the text may indeed mean that God will give *all the land* between the two rivers to Abram. As far as we know, the Israelites never possessed the land literally described, but we do know that a large population was understood as a blessing from God and that extensive land was required for a large population to survive.

The text implies, asserts actually, that the land given to Abraham's descendants was already possessed by others: Kenites, Kenizzites, Kadmonites, Hittites, Perizzites, Rephaim, Amorites, Canaanites, Girgashites, and Jebusites. As the extent of land cited might not have been intended literally, perhaps no literal meaning was intended in naming the peoples to be dispossessed. Some may have been dispossessed by non-Israelites (e.g., Rephaim); others seem to have become Israel's allies (e.g., Kenites).

To what extent the Israelites dispossessed people of their land, especially Canaanites and Jebusites, is difficult to answer. Biblical texts—for example, the Book of Joshua—would have us believe that the Israelites conquered all of Canaan and slaughtered all living there. The Book of Judges would have us believe, in contradictory fashion, that not all were slaughtered, and those not killed were subjected to forced labor. A historical reconstruction would suggest that the Israelites were not in position to conquer and that the biblical texts reflect a theological perspective, not a historical perspective. As such, the land symbolizes God's gift to the people as the means of their survival, proliferation, and prosperity— nothing more, nothing less.

### Genesis 17:7-8

> (7) I will establish my covenant between me and you, and
> your offspring after you throughout their generations, for an
> everlasting covenant, to be God to you and to your offspring
> after you. (8) And I will give to you, and to your offspring
> after you, the land where you are now an alien, all the land of
> Canaan, for a perpetual holding; and I will be their God."

This version of God's promised covenant with Abram follows
his change in name to Abraham, which means "father of a multitude" (v. 5). As already promised, his offspring will be many; thus,
his name now reflects God's promise more explicitly. The
covenant is made not only with Abraham but with his descendants
and will last through the generations. The *relationship* of God to
Abraham and his descendants is articulated as essential to any
notion of covenant: God promises to be God for Abraham and his
offspring.

Additionally, but not as an afterthought, God promises to give
Abraham and his descendants the land on which Abraham now
dwells as an alien, that is, the land of Canaan. Though the size of
Abraham's family and its duration are integral to the text, there is
no effort to provide defense for the land Abraham will receive.
Rather, the focus is on Abraham coming to possess the land on
which he now lives. The broader context is God's covenant relationship with Abraham and his descendants through time.

## Inherited Land

### Genesis 48:4

> And [God] said to me [Jacob], "I am going to make you
> fruitful and increase your numbers; I will make of you a
> company of peoples, and will give this land to your offspring
> after you for a perpetual holding."

In Genesis 12 God promises land to Abram. Subsequent texts
reiterate the promise and extend it to Abraham's son Isaac and his
descendants (Gen. 24:7) and to Isaac's son Jacob and his descendants (Gen. 28:13). In Gen. 48:4 Jacob refers to that promise while

claiming his son Joseph's two sons, Ephraim and Manasseh, as his own. They will inherit their share of the land God has promised to Jacob and his descendants. God had caused Jacob to be fruitful and said his descendants would become a "company of peoples," who would inherit the land God had promised. The gift of a secured land increases dramatically the probability of the people's survival.

### *Deuteronomy 12:1*

> These are the statutes and ordinances that you must diligently observe in the land that the LORD, the God of your ancestors, has given you to occupy all the days that you live on the earth.

Deut. 12:1 introduces a body of law and practice that Moses enumerates within his farewell speech to the Israelites. Although some of the teachings may actually date to the monarchy, placement on the lips of Moses gives the teaching authority.

The text mentions appropriate behavior once the Israelites have entered the land of Canaan and during the time they live there. Describing the land as God's gift, the text suggests motivation for the Israelites' obedience to God's statutes and ordinances. The God who has given them the land has a history as their ancestors' God. The land also has a history, having been promised to their ancestors, and God intends that the land have a present and a future in relationship to the people. The text says *explicitly* that the Israelites are diligently to observe God's statutes and ordinances in the land promised. The text *implies* that diligent observance of God's statutes and ordinances will secure their occupation "all the days that [they] live on the earth." Again, we remind ourselves that possession of land is critical for the people's well-being; God has promised the land, and by implication, the potential for future well-being.

### *Deuteronomy 12:10*

> When you cross over the Jordan and live in the land that the LORD your God is allotting to you, and when he gives you rest from your enemies all around so that you live in safety . . .

Deut. 12:10, though not even a complete sentence, represents similar verses reiterating that the land is God's gift to the people. Although the allotted land is presented here on the other side of the Jordan, that is, west of the Jordan River, the people in fact come to possess land east of the Jordan as well (e.g., Deut. 3:12-13).

The land is a piece of the puzzle essential to ensuring the Israelites' continued survival and well-being. They need human fertility and the increase of livestock, both of which need the fruits of the field for food, that is, the produce of the land. The Israelites also need defense from enemies and a respite from violence. The text assures that God will provide for these needs.

## Of Milk and Honey
### Leviticus 20:24

> But I [God] have said to you: You shall inherit their land, and I will give it to you to possess, a land flowing with milk and honey. I am the Lord your God; I have separated you from the peoples.

The land God promises to the Israelites is the land they shall possess; it will be their inheritance after the Lord brings them into it. But inheritances differ: what kind of land is the Lord promising the people? The land here, and in many other biblical texts, is described as a "land flowing with milk and honey," that is, a fertile land. When humans and other animals have borne offspring, the female of the species is rich in milk with which to feed the newly born. A land that flows in milk is a land wherein all the animals are fertile.

But the land that the Lord promises to the Israelites is also a land in which other living beings are fertile. In a land flowing with honey the bees are plentiful and fruitful, and the food they produce is like the milk in that it, too, provides nourishment for animals. In this land the people—"a multitude" (see Gen. 17:4 above)—will be able to survive and multiply (see Gen. 1:28 and 9:7 above).

The separation mentioned in verse 24 alludes to God's promise of special protection, and refers to the people for whom God explicitly is identified as their God. All living beings will cooperate in God's plan for the well-being of God's people.

### Numbers 14:7-8

(7) And [Joshua and Caleb] said to all the congregation of the Israelites, "The land that we went through as spies is an exceedingly good land. (8) If the LORD is pleased with us, he will bring us into this land and give it to us, a land that flows with milk and honey."

According to the narrative, Moses sent spies to investigate the land across the Jordan, the land which the Lord had promised and which the people, for their part, hoped to possess. Although most of the spies presented a picture that would deter the Israelites from seeking to enter, Joshua and Caleb are faithful to the Lord's will and supportive of the Israelites moving into the land. They describe a land worthy of God's gift to a favored people, "an exceedingly good land."

Joshua and Caleb are aware of the conditional character of the gift, stating that the people will come to possess the land "if the LORD is pleased with [them]." The people's faithfulness to God is clearly a condition of receiving the promised gift, and the spies imply that the people should strive to remain in the Lord's favor. After all, in a time and place in which any land is worth possessing, this possession has exceptional value as a land "that flows with milk and honey."

### Deuteronomy 6:3

Hear therefore, O Israel, and observe them [the statutes and ordinances that the LORD charged Moses to teach the Israelites] diligently, so that it may go well with you, and so that you may multiply greatly in a land flowing with milk and honey, as the LORD, the God of your ancestors, has promised you.

Moses' so-called farewell speech to the Israelite people, on the brink of Canaan, admonishes them to obey the teachings that the

Lord had charged Moses to teach. Such faithfulness is, according to Moses, essential if all is to go well. This state of well-being extends to life in the land. The people's adherence to God's teachings is somehow connected to their own fertility and to the fertility of the land, which would, in turn, benefit the people. Everything works together: the Lord has promised the land; the people obey the Lord's teachings; the land—including all living things connected with it—produces abundantly for the people's sake. The drama does not just involve God and human beings but all of God's creation, and emphasizes the dependence and interdependence of human beings.

### Deuteronomy 11:8-9

> (8) Keep, then, this entire commandment that I am commanding you today, so that you may have strength to go in and occupy the land that you are crossing over to occupy, (9) and so that you may live long in the land that the LORD swore to your ancestors to give them and to their descendants, a land flowing with milk and honey.

Again and again, the Bible asserts that faithfulness to the teachings that God has given through Moses is critical to the people's well-being. The people need strength to enter and occupy the land which the Lord swore to their ancestors. The needed strength and endurance is linked to their faithful observance of God's teachings; the people cannot enter and occupy the land on their own. They must be fully faithful to the commands of God.

In addition to God's gift and the people's faithfulness, also implied as a prerequisite for sustainability is the land's fertility. The text depicts a land "flowing with milk and honey" so that the people can remain or, all things being equal, can remain "if" they are faithful to the Lord's command. The character of the land will not be detrimental to the people's endurance. The phrase "flowing with milk and honey" rather assures that the land can provide the food and water needed for the people to survive and grow.

### Deuteronomy 31:20

> For when I have brought them into the land flowing with milk and honey, which I promised on oath to their ancestors, and they have eaten their fill and grown fat, they will turn to other gods and serve them, despising me and breaking my covenant.

The fecund land that the Lord had promised the people and in which they would dwell would, unfortunately, become the locus of their unfaithfulness. When their needs and desires were satisfied, God predicts through Moses, the people would become idolators. What irony! With God consistently associated with the people's well-being, they will betray the covenant relationship in a state of satiety. Instead of loving or fearing God, instead of humble gratitude, they will turn to other gods, abandon their God, even "despise" their God. Despising God is synonymous with "breaking" God's covenant. The land, people, animals, and crops would be fertile, but God predicts through Moses that the fertility will lead to independence from the God of the covenant. Satiation will lead to infidelity.

## Filled with Abundance

### Deuteronomy 6:10-12

> (10) When the LORD your God has brought you into the land that he swore to your ancestors, to Abraham, to Isaac, and to Jacob, to give you—a land with fine, large cities that you did not build, (11) houses filled with all sorts of goods that you did not fill, hewn cisterns that you did not hew, vineyards and olive groves that you did not plant—and when you have eaten your fill, (12) take care that you do not forget the LORD, who brought you out of the land of Egypt, out of the house of slavery.

The land that the Lord has promised is frequently described as "a land flowing with milk and honey" (see above). While that description may have been intended literally, it was definitely intended symbolically: the land into which God would bring the people and that the Lord had sworn to give to Israel's ancestors would be fertile, supporting people, animals, and plants—the increase of all living beings. The land in Deut. 6:10-12 is also described as desirable, due to the output of fruit in relation to toil. The land would contain fruit-bearing vines and olive trees that the people didn't plant but from which they could eat. They could dwell in large cities they did not build. Their houses would be filled with good things without their having had to fill them, and the people would not have to carve stones to make cisterns; the cisterns would already have been carved out. The description clearly implies that the Israelites would take control of a land that had belonged to others, a land others cultivated and cared for. How will the Israelites take possession of the land? By conquest? By slow infiltration? By rapid or slow, but steady, domination? On these questions the text is curiously silent.

In fact, the text is not concerned with the acquisition of land, or with the satiation the land will provide. Rather, Deut. 6:12 warns of the Israelites' response once they have acquired the toil-free land and of the potential danger in such opulence. When all needs are satisfied, and satisfied abundantly, the people might be tempted to "forget" the Lord. The text reminds them that the Lord brought them out of slavery and bondage; they are warned not to forget that, ultimately, they depend on the God who has delivered them from Egypt and who has made abundance possible.

### Deuteronomy 7:13-15

> (13) He [God] will love you, bless you, and multiply you; he will bless the fruit of your womb and the fruit of your ground, your grain and your wine and your oil, the increase of your cattle and the issue of your flock, in the land that he swore to your ancestors to give you. (14) You shall be the most blessed of peoples, with neither sterility nor barrenness among you or your livestock. (15) The LORD will turn away from you every illness; all the dread diseases of Egypt that you experienced, he will not inflict on you, but he will lay them on all who hate you.

The Hebrew word for love is associated with covenant faithfulness. God's love is assumed for the people with whom God has made a covenant, who, in turn, are to love God and be faithful to their covenant identity. From the beginning, Israel's God has promised to bless the people (e.g., Gen. 12:2-3), a blessing that here is specified as multiplication. People, produce, grain, wine, and oil shall increase; herds and flocks will increase. None of the living creatures will be barren, and none will suffer from disease. This is how the text depicts life for the people to whom God had promised land.

### Deuteronomy 8:7-10

> (7) For the LORD your God is bringing you into a good land, a land with flowing streams, with springs and underground waters welling up in valleys and hills, (8) a land of wheat and barley, of vines and fig trees and pomegranates, a land of olive trees and honey, (9) a land where you may eat bread without scarcity, where you will lack nothing, a land whose stones are iron and from whose hills you may mine copper. (10) You shall eat your fill and bless the LORD your God for the good land that he has given you.

The text is self-explanatory. The land into which the people will go is a good land, defined as a land on which life can be sustained and even prosper. Such land contains flowing streams, springs, underground water sources, and soil conducive to the harvest of wheat and barley and to the growth of grape-bearing vines and fig and olive-bearing fruit trees—essential food products are not scarce. To enhance the value and utility of the land, its stone is rich in iron and copper. The text assumes that the people acknowledge God as the One responsible for their dwelling place. It is appropriate, therefore, for the people to bless and thank the Lord.

### Deuteronomy 11:11-12, 14-15

> (11) But the land that you are crossing over to occupy is a land of hills and valleys, watered by rain from the sky, (12) a land that the LORD your God looks after. The eyes of the LORD your God are always on it, from the beginning of the year to the end of the year. . . .
> (14) [T]hen he [God] will give the rain for your land in its season, the early rain and the later rain, and you will

gather in your grain, your wine, and your oil; (15) and he
will give grass in your fields for your livestock, and you will
eat your fill.

These verses credit God explicitly with the fertility of the land
the people are about to enter. Described with "hills and valleys,"
the land receives the water necessary to generate seeds in arable
soil. God provides the water by providing rain and, moreover,
takes care of the land from the beginning of the year to its end. The
seasons provide early rain and late rain, planting rain and harvest
rain to guarantee the fertility of grain, wine, and oil, which
humans need, and of field grasses on which livestock graze. All
works together for good: land when watered becomes arable;
seeds, when planted in arable soil and watered by rain, grow; crops
when harvested become food for humans, field grasses become
food for other animals; and water quenches the thirst of all. The
Lord gives an interdependent, life-giving land, a land in which
people not only survive, but thrive. Such is the people's understanding of the gift.

### Deuteronomy 28:3-5, 8, 11-12

(3) Blessed shall you be in the city, and blessed shall you be
in the field.

(4) Blessed shall be the fruit of your womb, the fruit of
your ground, and the fruit of your livestock, both the
increase of your cattle and the issue of your flock.

(5) Blessed shall be your basket and your kneading bowl.
. . . (8) The LORD will command the blessing upon you in
your barns, and in all that you undertake. . . . (11) The LORD
will make you abound in prosperity, in the fruit of your
womb, in the fruit of your livestock, and in the fruit of your
ground in the land that the LORD swore to your ancestors to
give you. (12) The LORD will open for you his rich store-
house, the heavens, to give the rain of your land in its season
and to bless all your undertakings. . . .

Summarized in Deuteronomy 28 are God's gifts if the people follow obediently the teachings God has made known through Moses.

If they accept their identity as God's people with God as their covenant God, then God will provide abundantly for their well-being. The blessings God will provide include what the people need to survive, and their hopes and wishes in excess of needs. The list includes (1) God's providence everywhere—in city and field; (2) fertility of every thing—people, land, cattle, flocks; (3) an excess of food available for storage; (4) success in all undertakings; and (5) the heaven-sent gift of rain. If the elements essential to survival—including elements not under human control—were assured, then the people could relax and rejoice. Surely this list of God's blessings was intended to diminish the uncertainty and anxiety brought on by sterility, scarcity, and the fear of famine and drought.

## Sabbath for the Land

### Leviticus 25:1-7

> (1) The LORD spoke to Moses on Mount Sinai, saying: (2) Speak to the people of Israel and say to them: When you enter the land that I am giving you, the land shall observe a sabbath for the LORD. (3) Six years you shall sow your field, and six years you shall prune your vineyard, and gather in their yield; (4) but in the seventh year there shall be a sabbath of complete rest for the land, a sabbath for the LORD: you shall not sow your field or prune your vineyard. (5) You shall not reap the aftergrowth of your harvest or gather the grapes of your unpruned vine; it shall be a year of complete rest for the land. (6) You may eat what the land yields during its sabbath—you, your male and female slaves, your hired and your bound laborers who live with you; (7) for your livestock also, and for the wild animals in your land all its yield shall be for food.

In Lev. 25:1-7 the Priestly writers place on Mount Sinai the Lord's directive to Moses that the land itself was to observe a sabbath. In other texts, the Lord observes a sabbath after the works of creation (Gen. 2:2); the Lord's people, their slaves and animals, and resident aliens observe a sabbath in honor of the Lord's rest at creation (Exod. 20:8-11); the Lord's people and all living beings in their charge observe a sabbath so that the slaves may rest (Deut. 5:12-14). Here, the Lord's people observe a sabbath so that the land itself may rest. Not every seventh day, but every seventh year, the land shall have rest.

What work does the land do that it needs rest? The text describes the land's work of accepting the seed and producing the vines for the harvest. If God, God's people, and the slaves and animals belonging to God's people rest, surely the land that nourishes God's people with food must also need and receive rest. The interconnectedness is obvious. The food that the land yields without being worked or disturbed may indeed provide food for all the people and their animals, but the text insists that the land have rest.

## The Extent of the Land
### Numbers 34:1-12

(1) The LORD spoke to Moses, saying: (2) Command the Israelites, and say to them: When you enter the land of Canaan (this is the land that shall fall to you for an inheritance, the land of Canaan, defined by its boundaries), (3) your south sector shall extend from the wilderness of Zin along the side of Edom. Your southern boundary shall begin from the end of the Dead Sea on the east; (4) your boundary shall turn south of the ascent of Akrabbim, and cross to Zin, and its outer limit shall be south of Kadesh-barnea; then it shall go on to Hazar-addar, and cross to Azmon; (5) the boundary shall turn from Azmon to the Wadi of Egypt, and its termination shall be at the Sea.

(6) For the western boundary, you shall have the Great Sea and its coast; this shall be your western boundary.

(7) This shall be your northern boundary: from the Great Sea you shall mark out your line to Mount Hor; (8) from Mount Hor you shall mark it out to Lebo-hamath, and the outer limit of the boundary shall be at Zedad; (9) then the boundary shall extend to Ziphron, and its end shall be at Hazar-enan; this shall be your northern boundary.

(10) You shall mark out your eastern boundary from Hazar-enan to Shepham; (11) and the boundary shall con-

tinue down from Shepham to Riblah on the east side of Ain;
and the boundary shall go down, and reach the eastern
slope of the sea of Chinnereth; (12) and the boundary shall
go down to the Jordan, and its end shall be at the Dead Sea.
This shall be your land with its boundaries all around.

Though the Pentateuch in several places describes the extent of
the land promised by God, Num. 34:1-12 is perhaps one of the
most detailed passages. Each boundary is delineated in every
direction, the description suggesting that the boundaries of
Israel's territory fall within the land of Canaan, a less extensive territory than that implied in other texts. But because of their detail,
the verses make the acquisition and occupation more definite,
indicating actual boundaries in place during Israel's early history.

### Deuteronomy 11:24

Every place on which you set foot shall be yours; your territory shall extend from the wilderness to the Lebanon and
from the River, the river Euphrates, to the Western Sea.

This verse, despite its brevity, offers a different version of the
land's extent. The first part of the verse sets the boundary not by
geographical limits, but by unlimited possibility. The verse is
sweeping: "every place on which you set foot . . ." The remainder
of the verse sets the limits: from the wilderness, that is, the desert,
in the south, to Lebanon in the north, and from the Euphrates
River in the east to the Mediterranean Sea in the west. The experience is of vastness and possibility, the territorial vagueness contributing to a sense of the land's expanse. Implicit in the expanse
is a sense of hope; there is room for the land's fertility and, as a
direct consequence, for the people's prosperity.

## Distributing the Land

### Numbers 26:52-56

(52) The LORD spoke to Moses, saying: (53) To these the
land shall be apportioned for inheritance according to the
number of names. (54) To a large tribe you shall give a large

inheritance, and to a small tribe you shall give a small inheritance; every tribe shall be given its inheritance according to its enrollment. (55) But the land shall be apportioned by lot; according to the names of their ancestral tribes they shall inherit. (56) Their inheritance shall be apportioned according to lot between the larger and the smaller.

Numbers 26 lists the names of the people twenty years of age and older said to have come out with Moses from Egypt. The list is arranged by clans, families of the sons of Jacob, and includes Reuben, Simeon, Gad, Judah, Issachar, Zebulun, Joseph, Ephraim, Benjamin, Dan, Asher, and Naphtali. Each clan is to receive a portion of the land promised to the Israelites. The listing also includes the sons of Levi, though they will not receive an allotment. While the chapter names several descendants of each clan, and thus implies that some clans have more descendants than others, the text names only a small representation of what is said to be the total number of Israelites.

The chapter does not specify which area will be allotted to which clan, but asserts that that decision will be made by lot, apparently to avoid favoritism. Obviously, some land—arable, with rich soil, located near water—is preferable to other land. Such land is more likely to produce food, which will enable people and animals to survive and thrive.

Numbers 26 specifies that larger clans will receive more land than smaller clans, seemingly in keeping with the fairness the lots sought to provide. No individual or group was to receive a larger per capita portion of land than another. Each would have an equal portion, insofar as its portion would correspond to its size. Each group would keep the portion determined by lots.

### Numbers 32:33

Moses gave to them—to the Gadites and to the Reubenites and to the half-tribe of Manasseh son of Joseph—the kingdom of King Sihon of the Amorites and the kingdom of King Og of Bashan, the land and its towns, with the territories of the surrounding towns.

The Gadites, the Reubenites, and the Manassites, that is, the descendants of Joseph's son Manasseh, were allotted the land east of the Jordan River, the land formerly occupied by the kindoms of Sihon and Og, the lands of the Amorites and Bashan. Their allotment included the land, its towns, and the territories of the surrounding towns. The following verses name cities that the Israelites rebuilt and cities they captured and incorporated as their own.

### Numbers 33:53-54

(53) You shall take possession of the land and settle in it, for I have given you the land to possess. (54) You shall apportion the land by lot according to your clans; to a large one you shall give a large inheritance, and to a small one you shall give a small inheritance; the inheritance shall belong to the person on whom the lot falls; according to your ancestral tribes you shall inherit.

These two verses resemble 26:52-56 above. They are not, however, part of a chapter dealing with a census; rather, chapter 33 contains a narrative history of Israel's journey from Egypt. The chapter concludes with directions for the Israelites entering and occupying Canaan, including the conditions according to which the newly acquired land is to be distributed.

The land is the promised treasure, containing the means whereby the Israelites can hope to survive and thrive; the land's quantitative distribution (proportionally equal) and its qualitative distribution (by lot) are designed to ensure that occupying the land will not become a source of contention.

# Part Two

# 4

# Sin: The Legitimation of Patriarchy

## Judgment

### Genesis 3:8-19

> (8) They [the first man and woman] heard the sound of the
> LORD God walking in the garden at the time of the evening
> breeze, and the man and his wife hid themselves from the
> presence of the LORD God among the trees of the garden.
> (9) But the LORD God called to the man, and said to him,
> "Where are you?" (10) He said, "I heard the sound of you in
> the garden, and I was afraid, because I was naked; and I hid
> myself."

In Genesis 3, the narrative unfolds of the serpent who per-
suades the woman to eat fruit from the tree of the knowledge of
good and evil, fruit that God had commanded the man not to eat.
Having eaten the fruit, the man and woman become aware of their
nakedness before God and are afraid; they hide. But when God
calls, the man answers and admits his fear.

> (11) He said, "Who told you that you were naked? Have you
> eaten from the tree of which I commanded you not to eat?"

God asks the man two more questions: How has the man come
to know that he is naked? Has he eaten from the forbidden tree?

> (12) The man said, "The woman whom you gave to be with me, she gave me fruit from the tree, and I ate."

The man never seems to answer directly. He had not told God, except perhaps by the direction from which his voice came, of his location in the garden. Now he does not answer questions about his nakedness or about having eaten from the forbidden tree. Perhaps the man assumes that God knows the answers, that God's questions are rhetorical. He asserts that the woman, God's gift to him, gave him fruit and that he ate. The man replies, in other words, that if you, God, had not given me the woman, and if she had not given me the fruit, I would not have eaten the fruit you told me not to eat.

> (13) Then the LORD God said to the woman, "What is this that you have done?" The woman said, "The serpent tricked me, and I ate."

Like the man, the woman begs the question. She blames the serpent for tricking her into eating the fruit and, also important, blames him for making the fruit sound irresistible, not just for giving it to her. Yet the fruit did not measure up to the serpent's promise; the serpent had lied.

> (14) The LORD God said to the serpent, "Because you have done this, cursed are you among all animals and among all wild creatures; upon your belly you shall go, and dust you shall eat all the days of your life. (15) I will put enmity between you and the woman, and between your offspring and hers; he will strike your head, and you will strike his heel." (16) To the woman he said, "I will greatly increase your pangs in childbearing; in pain you shall bring forth children, yet your desire shall be for your husband, and he shall rule over you."

The Lord curses the serpent for his part in the couple's disobedience. The serpent will crawl on its belly and eat dust and shall have an adverse relationship to the earth and a hostile relationship with human beings. Humans shall strike serpents, and serpents shall bite human beings.

Having cursed the serpent, the Lord punishes the woman. She will experience increased pain during pregnancy and childbirth. The pain might deter her from becoming pregnant, except that God will cause her to desire the one, her husband, who will make her pregnant. As further punishment, the Lord proclaims that the man will rule over the woman. These contradictions—the longing, pain, and domination—result from her misbehavior.

> (17) And to the man he said, "Because you have listened to the voice of your wife, and have eaten of the tree about which I commanded you, 'You shall not eat of it,' cursed is the ground because of you; in toil you shall eat of it all the days of your life; (18) thorns and thistles it shall bring forth for you; and you shall eat the plants of the field. (19) By the sweat of your face you shall eat bread until you return to the ground, for out of it you were taken; you are dust, and to dust you shall return."

The man had listened to the woman instead of God and would face the punishment of difficult and even life-threatening work to survive.

While God's judgment extends to all the perpetrators of unfaithfulness—animal life, woman, and man—and their punishments result in disharmony, the narrative legitimates patriarchy. The man rules over the woman, creating a social organization in which men dominate women.

Although Genesis condemns patriarchy insofar as it punishes the woman's behavior, and clearly perverts God's original intent for harmony between the sexes, Genesis 3 for the most part explains why things are the way they are. It is an etiological narrative. Enmity exists between human beings and certain animals; women experience pain in childbearing and are attracted to the very men who will dominate them; and men must engage in difficult and stressful work to secure food and survival. Patriarchy clearly does not represent relationships as they should be, but relationships as they commonly are, and as society has come to expect and even support.

# Genealogies

### Genesis 5:1-7, 28-30

> (1) This is the list of the descendants of Adam. When God created humankind, he made them in the likeness of God. (2) Male and female he created them, and he blessed them and named them "Humankind" when they were created.
>
> (3) When Adam had lived one hundred thirty years, he became the father of a son in his likeness, according to his image, and named him Seth. (4) The days of Adam after he became the father of Seth were eight hundred years; and he had other sons and daughters. (5) Thus all the days that Adam lived were nine hundred thirty years; and he died.
>
> (6) When Seth had lived one hundred five years, he became the father of Enosh. (7) Seth lived after the birth of Enosh eight hundred seven years, and had other sons and daughters. . . .
>
> (28) When Lamech had lived one hundred eighty-two years, he became the father of a son; (29) he named him Noah, saying, "Out of the ground that the Lord has cursed this one shall bring us relief from our work and from the toil of our hands." (30) Lamech lived after the birth of Noah five hundred ninety-five years, and had other sons and daughters.

Patriarchy is established and reinforced in part by identifying families with fathers as their heads. God made Adam's descendants "male and female" (v. 2), though in the delineation of descendants that follows Adam fathers Seth and other "sons and daughters." The genealogy wishes to name one of Adam's sons and then, while others remain unnamed, to indicate generically that he was not Adam's only child. Adam's unnamed daughters remain unremembered as individuals and, in contrast to Seth, invisible.

Like Adam, Seth is recorded as fathering a son, Enosh. The genealogy indicates that Seth fathered other children—sons and daughters—in addition to Enosh. But Seth's daughters, like Adam's, remain unnamed, unidentified, and undifferentiated.

Verses 8-27 function like the chapter's first seven verses. Enosh fathers Kenan, and other sons and daughters (vv. 9-10); Kenan fathers Mahalalel, and other sons and daughters (vv. 12-13); Mahalalel fathers Jared, and other sons and daughters (vv. 15-16); Jared fathers Enoch, and other sons and daughters (vv. 18-19); Enoch fathers Methuselah, and other sons and daughters (vv. 21-22); Methuselah fathers Lamech, and other sons and daughters (vv. 25-26). In each case, a father named and identified as his father's son begets a son who is named and who becomes the father of another named son. Each son (perhaps the firstborn?) has siblings, male and female, but the text deprives all of the females of names. Even their identity related to men—as daughters and mothers—is denied.

Lamech fathers Noah, who not only is named but whose name is explained with clear reference to the judgment in Genesis 3, where the Lord had cursed the ground and inflicted difficult work and toil on men (v. 17). The male offspring of Lamech, Noah, would now bring relief. The name foreshadows the new creation and the covenant God will make with all creation in Genesis 9.

### Genesis 10:1-4, 6-8, 13-18, 22-29

> (1) These are the descendants of Noah's sons, Shem, Ham, and Japheth; children were born to them after the flood. (2) The descendants of Japheth: Gomer, Magog, Madai, Javan, Tubal, Meshech, and Tiras. (3) The descendants of Gomer: Ashkenaz, Riphath, and Togarmah. (4) The descendants of Javan: Elishah, Tarshish, Kittim, and Rodanim. . . .
>
> (6) The descendants of Ham: Cush, Egypt, Put, and Canaan. (7) The descendants of Cush: Seba, Havilah, Sabtah, Raamah, and Sabteca. The descendants of Raamah: Sheba and Dedan. (8) Cush became the father of Nimrod; he was the first on earth to become a mighty warrior. . . . (13) Egypt became the father of Ludim, Anamim, Lehabim, Naphtuhim, (14) Pathrusim, Casluhim, and Caphtorim, from which the Philistines come.
>
> (15) Canaan became the father of Sidon his firstborn, and Heth, (16) and the Jebusites, the Amorites, the Girgashites, (17) the Hivites, the Arkites, the Sinites, (18) the Arvadites, the Zemarites, and the Hamathites. Afterward the families of the Canaanites spread abroad. . . .

. . . (22) The descendants of Shem: Elam, Asshur,
Arpachshad, Lud, and Aram. (23) The descendants of Aram:
Uz, Hul, Gether, and Mash. (24) Arpachshad became the
father of Shelah; and Shelah became the father of Eber. (25)
To Eber were born two sons: the name of the one was Peleg,
for in his days the earth was divided, and his brother's name
was Joktan. (26) Joktan became the father of Almodad,
Sheleph, Hazarmaveth, Jerah, (27) Hadoram, Uzal, Diklah,
(28) Obal, Abimael, Sheba, (29) Ophir, Havilah, and Jobab;
all these were the descendants of Joktan.

Among the many genealogies in the Pentateuch, Genesis 10 is
of particular interest. Taking up where the genealogy in Genesis 5
leaves off, Genesis 10 traces the descendants of Noah, though, in
contrast to the earlier genealogy, the chapter lacks reference to
fathers' daughters. In fact, although the NRSV translates that
"children" were born to Noah's sons after the flood, the Hebrew
says only that "sons" were born. Again in contrast to Genesis 5,
more than one son is named. The names of many of the sons are
eponymous, that is, they refer not to individuals but to peoples:
coastland peoples (v. 5); Philistines (v. 14); Jebusites, Amorites,
and Girgashites (v. 16); Hivites, Arkites, and Sinites (v. 17); and
Arvadites, Zemarites, and Hamathites (v. 18). The text names
these peoples to assert that the new creation—the descendants of
Noah after the flood—spread over the earth. While the fathering
of families requires fertile females, the names of these women—
even a general reference to them as wives and mothers—are noto-
riously absent.

### Genesis 11:10-25, 27

(10) These are the descendants of Shem. When Shem was
one hundred years old, he became the father of Arpachshad
two years after the flood; (11) and Shem lived after the birth
of Arpachshad five hundred years, and had other sons and
daughters.
(12) When Arpachshad had lived thirty-five years, he
became the father of Shelah; (13) and Arpachshad lived
after the birth of Shelah four hundred three years, and had
other sons and daughters.

(14) When Shelah had lived thirty years, he became the father of Eber; (15) and Shelah lived after the birth of Eber four hundred three years, and had other sons and daughters.

(16) When Eber had lived thirty-four years, he became the father of Peleg; (17) and Eber lived after the birth of Peleg four hundred thirty years, and had other sons and daughters.

(18) When Peleg had lived thirty years, he became the father of Reu; (19) and Peleg lived after the birth of Reu two hundred nine years, and had other sons and daughters.

(20) When Reu had lived thirty-two years, he became the father of Serug; (21) and Reu lived after the birth of Serug two hundred seven years, and had other sons and daughters.

(22) When Serug had lived thirty years, he became the father of Nahor; (23) and Serug lived after the birth of Nahor two hundred years, and had other sons and daughters.

(24) When Nahor had lived twenty-nine years, he became the father of Terah; (25) and Nahor lived after the birth of Terah one hundred nineteen years, and had other sons and daughters. . . .

(27) Now these are the descendants of Terah. Terah was the father of Abram, Nahor, and Haran; and Haran was the father of Lot.

The genealogy in Genesis 11 traces the descendants of Noah's oldest son, Shem, and distances, by generations and therefore by years, the ancestor Noah from his descendants Abram, Nahor, and Haran. The Genesis 11 genealogy shares the format of Genesis 5, first naming a father who begets a named son, and then indicating that the father had other sons and daughters. The genealogy establishes or at least suggests the extent of the familial line. Although a family line obviously cannot be established and maintained, let alone strengthened and enlarged, without the active intervention of women as wives and mothers, the patriarchal character of the Genesis genealogies, and presumably of ancient Israel, excluded any mention of females except when needed to differentiate the patrilineal line.

### Genesis 35:22b-26

> (22b) Now the sons of Jacob were twelve. (23) The sons of
> Leah: Reuben (Jacob's firstborn), Simeon, Levi, Judah,
> Issachar, and Zebulun. (24) The sons of Rachel: Joseph
> and Benjamin. (25) The sons of Bilhah, Rachel's maid: Dan
> and Naphtali. (26) The sons of Zilpah, Leah's maid: Gad
> and Asher. These were the sons of Jacob who were born to
> him in Paddan-aram.

The familiarity of the "twelve sons of Jacob" prompts the inclusion of these verses here, although the text does not go on to name the sons' sons. The verses occur after Rachel dies while giving birth to Benjamin. One notices how Jacob's sons are identified according to the woman who bore them. Leah's six sons are named first, then Rachel's two sons. Following are the sons of Leah's maid, Bilhah. Finally, the sons of Rachel's maid Zilpah are listed. The list does not order Jacob's sons according to their births, although Reuben is the firstborn. Jacob's wives have narrative import, which is reflected here.

What is troubling in this comprehensive naming is the absence of any reference to Jacob and Leah's daughter Dinah. Genesis 34 recounted the rape of Dinah, yet she is omitted in a following summary of Jacob's children. To be sure, she is never identified as ancestor to any of the tribes of Israel. The patriarchy dominating the text at this point, and which undoubtedly dominated the consciousness of ancient Israel, omits, except in unusual cases, women's names from genealogies, depriving women of the credit that is their due for the necessary role they play in furthering Israel's tribes.

### Genesis 36:1-5, 9-14

> (1) These are the descendants of Esau (that is, Edom). (2)
> Esau took his wives from the Canaanites: Adah daughter of
> Elon the Hittite, Oholibamah daughter of Anah son of
> Zibeon the Hivite, (3) and Basemath, Ishmael's daughter,
> sister of Nebaioth. (4) Adah bore Eliphaz to Esau; Basemath
> bore Reuel; (5) and Oholibamah bore Jeush, Jalam, and
> Korah. These are the sons of Esau who were born to him in
> the land of Canaan. . . .

(9) These are the descendants of Esau, ancestor of the
Edomites, in the hill country of Seir. (10) These are the
names of Esau's sons: Eliphaz son of Adah the wife of Esau;
Reuel, the son of Esau's wife Basemath. (11) The sons of
Eliphaz were Teman, Omar, Zepho, Gatam, and Kenaz. (12)
(Timna was a concubine of Eliphaz, Esau's son; she bore
Amalek to Eliphaz.) These were the sons of Adah, Esau's
wife. (13) These were the sons of Reuel: Nahath, Zerah,
Shammah, and Mizzah. These were the sons of Esau's wife,
Basemath. (14) These were the sons of Esau's wife
Oholibamah, daughter of Anah son of Zibeon: she bore to
Esau Jeush, Jalam, and Korah.

Jacob's brother Esau marries outside the family. Whereas Jacob
returns to his mother's home to find a wife, Esau takes women
from Canaan, a practice his mother found unacceptable. In contrast to the genealogies that omit the names of Israelite women,
this genealogy names and identifies Esau's Canaanite wives: Adah,
the daughter of a Hittite, and Oholibamah, the daughter of a
Hivite. Basemath, though not a Canaanite, is the daughter of
Esau's rejected uncle, Ishmael.

In contrast to other biblical genealogies, this genealogy differen-
tiates among the sons of Esau according to the wife who bore each
child. The names of the wives/mothers are reiterated. Moreover, the
name of each son's son is also connected to women. For example,
Adah bore Eliphaz, and Eliphaz fathered five sons who are traced
back to their grandmother. Another of Eliphaz's sons is linked
explicitly to a named concubine, Timna. Basemath bore Reuel, and
Reuel bore four sons who also are traced back to their grandmother. The genealogy continues through verse 43, reiterating the names
and relationships of the women while establishing the proliferation
of the families into clans. Again in contrast to other genealogies, the
chapter suggests that some women may have had eponymous
names, for example, Timna (v. 40) and Oholibamah (v. 41). One
might conclude that in this genealogy Esau's wives perform the
function of male ancestors in other genealogies.

One can posit at least two hypotheses when asking why this
genealogy contrasts with others with respect to the naming of

women. The first hypothesis, acknowledging Esau's importance despite his problematic identity, concludes that the named women are included because they are daughters of significant foreign figures. These are not common women. Their fathers, also named, hold influential positions among the peoples to whom they belong. The second hypothesis suggests that the authors intended to diminish the importance of Esau's genealogy precisely by naming the women. Whereas other families proudly establish their lineage from father to son, Esau's lineage is complicated by the otherness of his wives, and implicitly by the otherness of his children, even his sons. After all, his people do not become Israelites; they are the "others," the Edomites. Most "others" do not warrant genealogies at all.

### Genesis 46:8-27

(8) Now these are the names of the Israelites, Jacob and his offspring, who came to Egypt. Reuben, Jacob's firstborn, (9) and the children of Reuben: Hanoch, Pallu, Hezron, and Carmi. (10) The children of Simeon: Jemuel, Jamin, Ohad, Jachin, Zohar, and Shaul, the son of a Canaanite woman. (11) The children of Levi: Gershon, Kohath, and Merari. (12) The children of Judah: Er, Onan, Shelah, Perez, and Zerah (but Er and Onan died in the land of Canaan); and the children of Perez were Hezron and Hamul. (13) The children of Issachar: Tola, Puvah, Jashub, and Shimron. (14) The children of Zebulum: Sered, Elon, and Jahleel (15) (these are the sons of Leah, whom she bore to Jacob in Paddan-aram, together with his daughter Dinah; in all his sons and his daughters numbered thirty-three). (16) The children of Gad: Ziphion, Haggi, Shuni, Ezbon, Eri, Arodi, and Areli. (17) The children of Asher: Imnah, Ishvah, Ishvi, Beriah, and their sister Serah. The children of Beriah: Heber and Malchiel (18) (these are the children of Zilpah, whom Laban gave to his daughter Leah; and these she bore to Jacob— sixteen persons). (19) The children of Jacob's wife Rachel: Joseph and Benjamin. (20) To Joseph in the land of Egypt were born Manasseh and Ephraim, whom Asenath daughter of Potiphera, priest of On, bore to him. (21) The children of Benjamin: Bela, Becher, Ashbel, Gera, Naanam, Ehi, Rosh,

Muppim, Huppim, and Ard (22) (these are the children of Rachel, who were born to Jacob—fourteen persons in all). (23) The children of Dan: Hashum. (24) The children of Naphtali: Jahzeel, Guni, Jezer, and Shillem (25) (these are the children of Bilhah, whom Laban gave to his daughter Rachel, and these she bore to Jacob—seven persons in all). (26) All the persons belonging to Jacob who came into Egypt, who were his own offspring, not including the wives of his sons, were sixty-six persons in all. (27) The children of Joseph, who were born to him in Egypt, were two; all the persons of the house of Jacob who came into Egypt were seventy.

Just as the genealogy in Genesis 5 prepared the reader for the story of Noah, and the genealogy in Genesis 10–11 prepared the reader for the story of Abram, the genealogy in Genesis 46 prepares the reader for the story of the family of Jacob in Egypt.

In contrast to the listing of Jacob's sons in Genesis 36, this genealogy begins by listing a son of Jacob (e.g., Reuben) and then lists his sons by name. Only when six sons and their sons have been listed does the text identify the men as the sons whom Leah bore to Jacob. The sons clearly take precedence over the mother who bore them. The listing includes two other women, a Canaanite woman with whom Simeon fathered a son, and Dinah, Jacob and Leah's daughter. Reference is made to the fact that Jacob and Leah's "sons and daughters" numbered thirty-three, but thirty-three men's names—excluding Dinah from the count—are listed.

The genealogy names two more of Jacob's sons and their sons before identifying the men as sons of their mother Zilpah. The text does specify that Jacob's son Asher bore a daughter Serah; moreover, she is counted among the persons associated with Zilpah.

The genealogy then changes format, first naming Rachel and then identifying her as the mother of two sons, each of whom fathered sons. The genealogy notes that a named Egyptian woman, Asenath, most likely identified because of her status, fathered Joseph's sons. This positioning of Rachel may be a subtle indication of Jacob's preference for her.

Finally, the text names Jacob's last two sons and their sons, identified as sons of Rachel's maid Bilhah. When Jacob's family is totaled—including Leah and Zilpah, Rachel and Bilhah, but excluding their sons' wives—the number is seventy, symbolic of completion. Because of its attentiveness to sons, patriarchy legitimates the exclusion of women.

In contrast to the listing of Jacob's family in Genesis 35 (see above), this genealogy places Zilpah's sons before Rachel's, though Rachel is clearly differentiated from the other women whose names follow the names of their sons.

This final genealogy in Genesis, though dominated overwhelmingly by males, does name women and, to an extent greater than other genealogies in the Pentateuch, credits them, with Jacob, as ancestors of Israelite families. Nevertheless, patriarchy dominates the genre of genealogy.

## My Wife/My Sister
### Genesis 12:10-19

> (10) Now there was a famine in the land. So Abram went down to Egypt to reside there as an alien, for the famine was severe in the land.

Immediately following God's directive to Abram, sending him to the land that the Lord would show him, and Abram's arrival with his family in Canaan, a famine forces Abram to Egypt in search of food and survival. The verse foreshadows Jacob's later journey to Egypt, where he discovers his son Joseph. That journey, too, was provoked by famine. The verse underscores the people's vulnerability and their dependence on the land's fertility, as well as the fragility of their survival.

> (11) When he was about to enter Egypt, he said to his wife Sarai, "I know well that you are a woman beautiful in appearance; (12) and when the Egyptians see you, they will say, 'This is his wife'; then they will kill me, but they will let you live. (13) Say you are my sister, so that it may go well with me because of you, and that my life may be spared on your account."

Abram tells Sarai that he knows she is "beautiful in appearance." He follows the compliment, however, by asserting his assumption that her beauty will lead to his death. As Abram's wife, Sarai is his possession, an attractive possession at that. Taking away his possession would be theft, a violation of ancient Near Eastern law; moreover, if adultery were knowingly committed, the probable punishment would have been death. If she were not his possession, she would exist as a woman "beautiful in appearance," available for betrothal to the right man. Recognizing his vulnerability, Abram requests that Sarai identify herself as his sister. Under the circumstances, he would stand to benefit from her beauty. Though the language is request rather than command, the power imbalance between them assures her consent.

> (14) When Abram entered Egypt the Egyptians saw that the woman was very beautiful. (15) When the officials of Pharaoh saw her, they praised her to Pharaoh. And the woman was taken into Pharaoh's house. (16) And for her sake he dealt well with Abram; and he had sheep, oxen, male donkeys, male and female slaves, female donkeys, and camels.

Events occur as Abram had predicted. The Egyptians recognize Sarai's beauty, and she is taken into Pharaoh's house. Because of her, Abram is well paid with animals.

> (17) But the LORD afflicted Pharaoh and his house with great plagues because of Sarai, Abram's wife.

A modern reader might expect this verse to read: "The Lord afflicted Abram and his house with great plagues because of Abram's deceit," or, "The Lord afflicted Abram and his house with great plagues because of Abram's abuse of and cruelty to his wife Sarai." But Abram is protected; rather than punishment falling to Abram for giving Sarai to Pharaoh, it falls to Pharaoh for having taken her. The verse alerts the reader to the fact that Sarai serves as a pawn in a narrative that is not about Sarai at all. Rather, the narrative concerns Abram and Pharaoh, specifically the Lord's *protection* of Abram and *punishment* of Pharaoh. The God of Abram holds power over all people.

> (18) So Pharaoh called Abram, and said, "What is this you
> have done to me? Why did you not tell me that she was your
> wife? (19) Why did you say, 'She is my sister,' so that I took
> her for my wife? Now then, here is your wife, take her, and
> be gone."

Abram previously had spoken to Sarai in imperative form;
Pharaoh now speaks to Abram with questions. Clearly Abram is in
charge. Whether or not Pharaoh intends the questions as rhetorical and presumes the answers, his final words to Abram are imperatives. What he had done he now tells Abram to do: to take Sarai.
As another pharaoh will do to the Hebrews following plagues in
Egypt, he sends Abram and Sarai away.

### Genesis 20:1-7, 10-13

> (1) From there Abraham journeyed toward the region of the
> Negeb, and settled between Kadesh and Shur. While residing
> in Gerar as an alien, (2) Abraham said of his wife Sarah,
> "She is my sister." And King Abimelech of Gerar sent and
> took Sarah.

While living as an alien, Abraham presents his wife as his sister.
While this protects Abraham as in Genesis 12, false identification
makes it possible for the king to take Abraham's "sister" for a wife.
In the hierarchical world of the ancient Near East, one presumes
that kings could choose which woman or women would be theirs.

> (3) But God came to Abimelech in a dream by night, and
> said to him, "You are about to die because of the woman
> whom you have taken; for she is a married woman."

Despite Abraham's responsibility for the deceit and its consequences, the Lord does not punish him. Rather, the Lord informs
the king that he is about to die, a punishment associated with
adultery in Deut. 22:22.

> (4) Now Abimelech had not approached her; so he said,
> "Lord, will you destroy an innocent people? (5) Did he not
> himself say to me, 'She is my sister'? And she herself said, 'He
> is my brother.' I did this in the integrity of my heart and the
> innocence of my hands."

The text presumes hierarchy at work in the king's understanding that he represents the people and that his death would mean the people's destruction. Abimelech pleads innocence; he has not yet committed adultery, nor was that his intention. He had every reason to believe that Sarah was Abraham's sister. Abraham had said that she was, and she had confirmed Abraham's word.

> (6) Then God said to him in the dream, "Yes, I know that you did this in the integrity of your heart; furthermore it was I who kept you from sinning against me. Therefore I did not let you touch her. (7) Now then, return the man's wife; for he is a prophet, and he will pray for you and you shall live. But if you do not restore her, know that you shall surely die, you and all that are yours."

The Lord's original words to Abimelech come as a warning, not as a prediction of what would happen. The Lord claims credit for keeping the king from committing adultery and then commands Abimelech to return Sarah. The Lord protected Abraham. The Lord protected Abimelech. Are we to imply that the Lord also protected Sarah? Clearly the Lord establishes a hierarchy, in which Abraham serves as a prophet who will pray for Abimelech. Though Abimelech is a king, and has been protected, he is clearly less important than Abraham. Unfortunately, Sarah seems to come in third!

> (10) And Abimelech said to Abraham, "What were you thinking of, that you did this thing?"

As Abimelech had asked questions of God, he now asks Abraham, identified as a prophet, why he had behaved as he did.

> (11) Abraham said, "I did it because I thought, There is no fear of God at all in this place, and they will kill me because of my wife. (12) Besides, she is indeed my sister, the daughter of my father but not the daughter of my mother; and she became my wife. (13) And when God caused me to wander from my father's house, I said to her, 'This is the kindness you must do me: at every place to which we come, say of me, He is my brother.'"

Abraham's response parallels the reasoning he gave to Sarai in Gen. 12:12 (see above). He adds a reference, however, to the foreignness of the place, that it lacks fear of God. Furthermore, Abraham explains that Sarah is, in fact, his sister, insofar as they share the same father. (The genealogical reference in Gen. 11:26 does not reinforce this statement.) Abraham then implies that the pretense was not unique, but that Abraham had told Sarah that she must identify herself as his sister wherever they traveled. Whether verse 13 is intended to explain the inclusion of the narrative in Gen. 12:10-19 is unclear. In any case, patriarchy and hierarchy dominate.

### Genesis 26:1, 6-11

> (1) Now there was a famine in the land, besides the former famine that had occurred in the days of Abraham. And Isaac went to Gerar, to King Abimelech of the Philistines.

Famine had forced Abraham to travel to Egypt for food (see Gen. 12:10-19 above); now another famine forces Isaac from the land. The prevalence of famine and the threat posed to survival are clear. Famine resulted in forced migration, which required people to become resident aliens in others' lands.

> (6) So Isaac settled in Gerar. (7) When the men of the place asked him about his wife, he said, "She is my sister"; for he was afraid to say, "My wife," thinking, "or else the men of the place might kill me for the sake of Rebekah, because she is attractive in appearance."

This third account of presenting one's wife as a sister both resembles and differs from details in the other accounts. Abram/Abraham and Sarai/Sarah are replaced here by Isaac and Rebekah. The accounts in Genesis 20 and 26 take place in Gerar, and both narratives report that the patriarch identified his wife as his sister. Genesis 12 and 26 both allude to the attractiveness of the patriarch's spouse. All of the accounts suggest that the husband expected to be killed because of his wife.

> (8) When Isaac had been there a long time, King Abimelech of the Philistines looked out of a window and saw him fondling his wife Rebekah.

In contrast to the other two accounts, in which God brings about the king's discovery that the woman is the patriarch's wife— in Genesis 12 with plagues and in Genesis 20 with a dream—this verse credits Abimelech himself with the discovery.

> (9) So Abimelech called for Isaac, and said, "So she is your wife! Why then did you say, 'She is my sister'?" Isaac said to him, "Because I thought I might die because of her." (10) Abimelech said, "What is this you have done to us? One of the people might easily have lain with your wife, and you would have brought guilt upon us."

Abimelech forcefully asserts his conclusion regarding the woman's identity and demands from Isaac an explanation, which Isaac provides. He also recognizes the potential consequences had he or one of his men lain with another man's wife. Isaac would have brought guilt upon the people.

> (11) So Abimelech warned all the people, saying, "Whoever touches this man or his wife shall be put to death."

Abimelech's warning protects his people from adultery and its consequences. It also protects Isaac, for no one is to touch him. In contrast to Genesis 12 and 20, in which God is directly involved and the patriarch is clearly represented as superior to the foreign ruler—despite the fact that the incidents take place within the ruler's territory—this version seems to highlight the character of the foreign king. In none of the accounts is the woman/wife, Sarai/Sarah or Rebekah, taken seriously. The matriarchs are subjected to the consequences of male power relationships and victimized by male dominance.

# Rape

### Genesis 34:1-2

> (1) Now Dinah the daughter of Leah, whom she had borne to Jacob, went out to visit the women of the region. (2) When Shechem son of Hamor the Hivite, prince of the region, saw her, he seized her and lay with her by force.

Most commentaries on the rape of Dinah define the literary unit as embracing the entire chapter. Such a judgment is possible but often diminishes the significance of the rape. Much of the chapter deals with the activities of the men in relation to the rape. Although Shechem is the rapist, his father Hamor intervenes in an effort to win Dinah as Shechem's wife. As the father of Dinah and the representative of his people, Jacob is the one understood to have been offended. Two of Dinah's brothers, Simeon and Levi, act to avenge Shechem's deed, while the men of Shechem ultimately pay for the offense committed by the son of the regional prince. With so many men involved the victim easily gets lost. It is for this reason that I focus on the chapter's first two verses.

Verse one sets the scene. Dinah, as is common with women in the Bible, is identified as a daughter. The text identifies her, however, as the daughter of a mother, not as a father's daughter, which is most uncommon. When men are identified as sons of a named mother, it is frequently because their fathers, who have more than one wife, are of high status; this situation is common among Israel's and Judah's kings. It then becomes important to differentiate between children by naming their mothers. Sometimes a child is more beloved for having been born of a more beloved wife. Such is the case with Solomon, the son of David and Bathsheba, in contrast to Adonijah, son of David and Haggith (1 Kings 2:13). In the verses at hand, the text may name the mother of Dinah because of the importance of Jacob, or to differentiate between the more beloved of Jacob's wives, Rachel, and the less beloved but more fertile Leah.

On the other hand, the association of Dinah with a woman may represent the author's attempt to diminish Dinah's importance. In any case, Dinah went to visit other women, quite an acceptable thing to do. Verse 2 shifts the action from Dinah to Shechem, identifying him as the son of the regional prince. He sees Dinah, seizes her, and rapes her. What she did was quite appropriate; what he did was inexcusable.

Though Deuteronomy 22 specifies laws concerning sexual relations, whether these laws were in effect when Genesis 34 was written is unclear. According to Deut. 22:25, if a man meets an *engaged* woman in the open country, seizes her, and lies with her he should die, but the woman would not have committed an offense punishable by death. Dinah's trip to visit the women of the region may mean that she was traveling in open country when she was accosted. On the other hand, there is no indication that she was engaged. Deut. 22:28 requires that the man who meets a woman who is *not engaged*, who seizes her and lies with her, shall pay fifty shekels to the young woman's father, marry her, and not ever divorce her. The penalty is contingent, however, on the presence of witnesses. The scenario described in Deut. 22:28 seems to be more applicable to Dinah and Shechem's circumstances.

Though contemporary readers recoil at the idea of a woman having to marry her rapist, in the culture that produced this text the laws provided a woman with status, the likelihood of respectable offspring, and the structure to ensure material well-being. Unfortunately, Dinah does not have the opportunity to become Shechem's wife. The narrative relates the power relations between the families and the peoples without further attention to the character of Dinah. The victim is thus, as is often the case in rape, doubly victimized.

## Rivalries between Females

### Genesis 16:1-6

> (1) Now Sarai, Abram's wife, bore him no children. She had an Egyptian slave-girl whose name was Hagar, (2a) and Sarai said to Abram, "You see that the LORD has prevented me from bearing children; go in to my slave-girl; it may be that I shall obtain children by her."

The situation of a barren woman in ancient Israel was tragic. A woman's status depended, while a daughter, on her father, but once married the evaluation of her worth shifted to her husband and to the sons whom she bore. If unable to bear children, she had failed her husband. Sarai acknowledges the Lord as the one who opens wombs, and since the Lord had not opened her womb she gives her maid to Abram as her surrogate, hoping to bear children through Hagar. The hierarchy spawned by patriarchy extends to the power relationships between free women and foreign slave-girls.

> (2b) And Abram listened to the voice of Sarai. (3) So, after Abram had lived ten years in the land of Canaan, Sarai, Abram's wife, took Hagar the Egyptian, her slave-girl, and gave her to her husband Abram as a wife. (4) He went in to Hagar, and she conceived; . . .

Notice the inclusion and the repetition. Abram obeyed Sarai. Sarai gave her slave-girl to Abram. Abram did what Sarai told him to do, and Hagar did what Sarai had intended: she conceived.

> . . . and when she saw that she had conceived, she looked with contempt on her mistress.

As is often the case, Sarai received more than she asked for. Yes, she hoped for a surrogate child through Hagar, and she was not disappointed. But she also received Hagar's contempt. This, the reader is led to believe, Sarai had not anticipated.

> (5) Then Sarai said to Abram, "May the wrong done to me be on you! I gave my slave-girl to your embrace, and when she saw that she had conceived, she looked on me with contempt. May the Lord judge between you and me!"

Sarai feels herself caught in the middle. She had acted on her husband's behalf in giving Hagar to Abram and had reason to expect that his esteem for her would increase, that her status would be enhanced. Yet instead she experienced diminution, and at the hands of a slave! No wonder she was angry with Abram. Her behavior had resulted in the son he wanted, but Sarai was having to pay a heavy price.

(6a) But Abram said to Sarai, "Your slave-girl is in your power; do to her as you please."

At least two interpretations are possible for Abram's response. Abram perhaps sympathized with Sarai's complaint, prompting him to distance himself from Hagar. This would explain Abram's reminder to Sarai that Hagar was, after all, her slave, and that Sarai had a right to deal with her slaves as she wished. Abram thus assumes and supports hierarchy.

The second reading is not so favorable toward Abram. It, too, assumes a situation of hierarchy, but recognizes that Abram actually pits the women against each other. Rather than reminding Sarai that Hagar is only a slave, and that her contempt means nothing, Abram furthers the wedge between the two women.

(6b) Then Sarai dealt harshly with her, and she ran away from her.

With Abram's support, perhaps even on his implicit suggestion, Sarai behaves cruelly toward her less powerful sister.

### Genesis 30:1, 14-16

(1) When Rachel saw that she bore Jacob no children, she envied her sister; and she said to Jacob, "Give me children, or I shall die!"

The opening verse sets the tone for the incidents to follow. Rachel's sister Leah has accomplished what wives wish for, having borne her husband sons. Rachel, on the other hand, has not, and she envies her fertile sister. In frustration she demands children from her husband, though what follows upholds the traditional view that it is God who opens the womb.

(14) In the days of wheat harvest Reuben went and found mandrakes in the field, and brought them to his mother Leah. Then Rachel said to Leah, "Please give me some of your son's mandrakes." (15) But she said to her, "Is it a small matter that you have taken away my husband? Would you take away my son's mandrakes also?" Rachel said, "Then he

may lie with you tonight for your son's mandrakes." (16)
When Jacob came from the field in the evening, Leah went
out to meet him, and said, "You must come in to me; for I
have hired you with my son's mandrakes." So he lay with her
that night.

The incident relates the tension between Jacob's wives, the two
sisters Rachel and Leah. While Leah can boast of fertility and children, Rachel has Jacob's favor and is his companion each night. As
it happens, mandrakes were considered an aphrodisiac, assisting
sexual arousal and potentially helpful in conception.

That Leah takes possession of the mandrakes through her son
emphasizes her fertility. She who already has produced sons now
acquires a substance making it possible to bear more. Rachel, desperate to become pregnant, requests some of her sister's mandrakes.

Leah's reply contains traces of anger and bitterness. Yes, she has
sons; yes, she has mandrakes; but she no longer enjoys her husband's companionship. Leah resents both Rachel and Jacob's
attraction to her and, therefore, declines Rachel's request.

Rachel, driven by desperation, persists. In exchange for the
mandrakes, she offers Leah what she knows Leah craves: an opportunity to spend the night with Jacob. Leah consents.

Leah is pathetic. Having bargained for her husband, she now
must confess these facts to him. Leah had paid for the right to
sleep with Jacob, as if he were a prostitute. But she has not in fact
paid him, but has paid his wife, her sister.

Rachel is also pathetic. She gives away her husband for mandrakes. If God has not opened her womb, perhaps the mandrakes
will.

Contemporary readers may conclude that the text exposes the
problems of polygamy. But even more troublesome is the portray-
al of two women envious and in desperate competition with each
other for the "things" patriarchy values: husbands and sons.

# A Levirate Marriage

### Genesis 38:6-11

> (6) Judah took a wife for Er his firstborn; her name was Tamar. (7) But Er, Judah's firstborn, was wicked in the sight of the LORD, and the LORD put him to death. (8) Then Judah said to Onan, "Go in to your brother's wife and perform the duty of a brother-in-law to her; raise up offspring for your brother."

The narrative opens with a father, Judah, taking a wife for his firstborn son. There is no indication that either the man, Er, or his bride, Tamar, was consulted. According to biblical texts, fathers usually orchestrated the marriages of their children—with or without their children's consent. For example, Abraham directed his servant to find a wife for Isaac; Isaac charged Jacob to take a wife from the home of his mother's brother; and Hamor tried to arrange his son Shechem's marriage to Jacob's daughter Dinah. Punishment for Er's wickedness was early death. Since long life was considered a blessing (e.g., Exod. 20:12), its opposite was a curse.

Jacob responded to Er's death by telling his son Onan to "perform the duty of a brother-in-law" to Tamar, and to father a son for his deceased brother. The practice of a brother marrying his dead brother's wife and fathering a son with her, or of a widow marrying her dead husband's brother and bearing a son, is known as levirate marriage, from the Latin *levir* ("husband's brother"). Jacob instructs his second son, Onan, to enter into this arrangement with Tamar.

> (9) But since Onan knew that the offspring would not be his, he spilled his semen on the ground whenever he went in to his brother's wife, so that he would not give offspring to his brother. (10) What he did was displeasing in the sight of the LORD, and he put him to death also.

One may conclude that levirate marriage was not always acceptable to the men involved. Not they, but their deceased brother, would be credited with fathering the first son. Onan, though willing to have sexual intercourse with Tamar, was not willing to father a son for his brother Er. Onan's behavior, like his brother's, was wicked; like his brother, he died.

> (11) Then Judah said to his daughter-in-law Tamar, "Remain a widow in your father's house until my son Shelah grows up"—for he feared that he too would die, like his brothers. So Tamar went to live in her father's house.

With both Er and Onan dead, it was appropriate that Judah give his son Shelah to Tamar. However, using Shelah's youth as an excuse, Judah told Tamar he was postponing the union. The narrator explains that Judah feared that his son Shelah would also die. A father, blind to his sons' wickedness, links the woman to the evil that has befallen them. For her part, Tamar obeys her father-in-law.

Without going further, the reader already has learned that these men leave much to be desired. Two are evil, punished by death for their wickedness. The other man is simply blind and blames a woman when men are at fault. He is guilty of patriarchal prejudice.

The remainder of the narrative details how an intelligent, courageous, and persevering Tamar, despite the obstacles her father-in-law puts in her way, fulfills the obligations of levirate marriage for her dead husband.

### Deuteronomy 25:5-10

> (5) When brothers reside together, and one of them dies and has no son, the wife of the deceased shall not be married outside the family to a stranger. Her husband's brother shall go in to her, taking her in marriage, and performing the duty of a husband's brother to her, (6) and the firstborn whom she bears shall succeed to the name of the deceased brother, so that his name may not be blotted out of Israel.

What Genesis 38 recounts in narrative, Deuteronomy 25 records in law. The teaching poses a case of brothers living together and explains the threefold purpose of the law: (1) to prevent the marriage of the dead man's widow to a stranger outside the family; (2) to provide a son for the dead brother; and (3) to prevent the dead man's name from being erased.

(7) But if the man has no desire to marry his brother's widow, then his brother's widow shall go up to the elders at the gate and say, "My husband's brother refuses to perpetuate his brother's name in Israel; he will not perform the duty of a husband's brother to me."

The law, in contrast to Genesis, provides a course of action if the dead man's brother does not wish to marry his brother's widow. The widow may approach the elders at the gate to acknowledge that her brother-in-law refuses to perform the obligation.

(8) Then the elders of his town shall summon him and speak to him. If he persists, saying, "I have no desire to marry her," (9) then his brother's wife shall go up to him in the presence of the elders, pull his sandal off his foot, spit in his face, and declare, "This is what is done to the man who does not build up his brother's house." (10) Throughout Israel his family shall be known as "the house of him whose sandal was pulled off."

The elders will take action. If the brother-in-law persists in refusing to marry his dead brother's widow, then she shall speak and act publicly against him, pulling off his sandal and spitting in his face. Furthermore, she shall explain her actions as appropriate for a man unwilling to look after his brother's house. That man and his family will be publicly known henceforth for his neglect and for the humiliation his dead brother's widow inflicted on him.

The regulation, although legislating embarrassment for the man who refuses to carry out this obligation and punishment intended to encourage adherence, nevertheless focuses on the males as main characters. Even when the woman speaks and acts publicly—an uncommon occurrence—her behavior aims to exhort the man toward compliance, or to punish him for non-compliance. Though she has power to shame her husband's family, the culture has deprived her of the power to choose whether she will remarry; she must remarry for her material well-being. The culture has also deprived her of the power to choose whom she will marry. A widow whose dead husband's brother is alive is hardly another man's first-choice bride. If her dead husband's brother refuses to comply with the levirate law, she almost certainly is deprived of the only means the culture provides for attaining a husband and, necessarily, of material well-being; further, she is deprived of the potential for future sons. Yet these aspects of the woman's dilemma are almost hidden in the regulation. The issue is male progeny understood as a patriarchal project.

## A Jealous Husband
### Numbers 5:11-31

> (11) The LORD spoke to Moses, saying: (12) Speak to the Israelites and say to them: If any man's wife goes astray and is unfaithful to him . . .

It is important to realize that "the Israelites" in the above verse is the NRSV translation for the Hebrew "the sons of Israel." The provision described is directed only to men.

> . . . (13) if a man has had intercourse with her but it is hidden from her husband, so that she is undetected though she has defiled herself, and there is no witness against her since she was not caught in the act; . . .

Note the emphasis on the responsibility the woman bears for the behavior. Although it is the man who "has had intercourse with her," it is the woman who "has defiled herself." The witness(es) would testify against *her;* she would be the one caught in the act.

> . . . (14) if a spirit of jealousy comes on him, and he is jealous of his wife who has defiled herself; or if a spirit of jealousy comes on him, and he is jealous of his wife, though she has not defiled herself; (15a) then the man shall bring his wife to the priest.

If the man should become jealous—whether or not there are grounds for his jealousy—he is entitled to bring his wife to the priest, that is, to identify her publicly as, either in probability or possibility, having been unfaithful.

> (15b) And he shall bring the offering required for her, one-tenth of an ephah of barley flour. He shall pour no oil on it and put no frankincense on it, for it is a grain offering of jealousy, a grain offering of remembrance, bringing iniquity to remembrance.

Similar to other situations in which the people of Israel come before the priests, the text stipulates an offering, one identified in this case as appropriate to jealousy and remembrance, intended to bring "iniquity to remembrance." If the woman were guilty of iniquity, the offering was meant to expose her guilt, to cause it to be remembered. One notes the absence of a reciprocal provision for a man whose wife "suspects" him of infidelity. In a culture that accepted polygamy, such a provision would have been out of place.

> (16) Then the priest shall bring her near, and set her before the LORD; (17) the priest shall taken holy water in an earthen vessel, and take some of the dust that is on the floor of the tabernacle and put it into the water. (18) The priest shall set the woman before the LORD, dishevel the woman's hair, and place in her hands the grain offering of remembrance, which is the grain offering of jealousy. In his own hand the priest shall have the water of bitterness that brings the curse.

Note that the "holy water" is "the water of bitterness," with the function of bringing the curse if the woman is found guilty. Usually water brings about ritual purification, but here it determines guilt.

> (19) Then the priest shall make her take an oath, saying, "If no man has lain with you, if you have not turned aside to uncleanness while under your husband's authority, be immune to this water of bitterness that brings the curse. (20) But if you have gone astray while under your husband's authority, if you have defiled yourself and some man other than your husband has had intercourse with you" . . .

Note closely the priest's prayer. If the woman is innocent, the water will have no ill effects; if she is guilty. . . . Again, one notes the disparity between descriptions of the woman's and man's actions: she will have "gone astray" and will have "defiled" herself; he will have had intercourse. The text describes his action factually, hers judgmentally. The patriarchal issue behind such condemnation is clear: she is under her husband's authority.

> . . . (21)—let the priest make the woman take the oath of the curse and say to the woman—"the LORD make you an execration and an oath among your people, when the LORD makes your uterus drop, your womb discharge; (22) now may this water that brings the curse enter your bowels and make your womb discharge, your uterus drop!" And the woman shall say, "Amen. Amen."

The woman suspected of infidelity receives the priest's oath of the curse; if found guilty, she will be disgraced and rendered incapable of conception and pregnancy. She is to admit her wrongdoing. Eventually she will drink "the water of bitterness."

> (23) Then the priest shall put these curses in writing, and wash them off into the water of bitterness. (24) He shall make the woman drink the water of bitterness that brings the curse, and the water that brings the curse shall enter her and cause bitter pain.

Before the woman drinks, the priest commits the curse to writing and washes the curses in the water. The water will cause her bitter pain if she is guilty. Whether the pain should be understood as physical, resulting from an upset stomach and bloating, or symbolic, signifying an end to childbearing, or both, is unclear.

> (25) The priest shall take the grain offering of jealousy out of the woman's hand, and shall elevate the grain offering before the LORD and bring it to the altar; (26) and the priest shall take a handful of the grain offering, as its memorial portion, and turn it into smoke on the altar, and afterward shall make the woman drink the water.

While the woman held the grain offering the priest had been holding the water. He takes the offering from the woman and burns a portion on the altar, after which she drinks.

> (27) When he has made her drink the water, then, if she has defiled herself and has been unfaithful to her husband, the water that brings the curse shall enter into her and cause bitter pain, and her womb shall discharge, her uterus drop, and the woman shall become an execration among her people. (28) But if the woman has not defiled herself and is clean, then she shall be immune and be able to conceive children.

The guilty woman receives the curse. The innocent woman, though she has been publicly humiliated, will not experience the curse's effects.

> (29) This is the law in cases of jealousy, when a wife, while under her husband's authority, goes astray and defiles herself, (30) or when a spirit of jealousy comes on a man and he is jealous of his wife; then he shall set the woman before the Lord, and the priest shall apply this entire law to her.

This text reiterates the procedure, which is said to apply whenever a man is jealous of his wife—whether or not she is guilty. The procedure is intended to determine guilt.

> (31) The man shall be free from iniquity, but the woman shall bear her iniquity.

The concluding verse underlines the procedure's inequality and patriarchal preference. The man—whether or not he has accused his wife wrongly—is free from iniquity; the woman, on the other hand, if guilty, receives public humiliation and a punishment perhaps more severe than death—infertility. If innocent, she has been forced to undergo a terrible ordeal without official acknowledgment of the injustice done.

# 5

# Sin: The Legitimation of Hierarchy

## Sibling Rivalry

### Genesis 4:1-5, 8-9

> (1) Now the man knew his wife Eve, and she conceived and bore Cain, saying, "I have produced a man with the help of the LORD." (2) Next she bore his brother Abel. Now Abel was a keeper of sheep, and Cain a tiller of the ground. (3) In the course of time Cain brought to the LORD an offering of the fruit of the ground, (4) and Abel for his part brought of the firstlings of his flock, their fat portions. And the LORD had regard for Abel and his offering, (5) but for Cain and his offering he had no regard. So Cain was very angry, and his countenance fell.

When Adam "knows" Eve she conceives and bears a son. Eve's first son is Cain, a farmer. Her second son, Abel, is a shepherd. In due course the two sons bring offerings to the Lord; there is no indication that they were fulfilling an obligation. Cain offers some of his field's produce, without explicit indication that they were the first fruits of his harvest. Abel, on the other hand, is said explicitly to offer the lambs that opened the wombs of his sheep (cf. Exod. 34:19; Lev. 27:26). That Abel offered the fat portions may confirm the appropriateness of his offering. The text indicates that Abel's offering met with God's acceptance and approval, while Cain's did not. An obligation derived from the law to offer "first fruits" in Exod. 23:16, 19, and Lev. 23:10-14, may have been enforced when the passage was written, in which case the original recipients of the Genesis narrative would have understood that only Abel acted faithfully. Or, the original recipients may have understood the fact that the ground had been cursed (Gen. 3:17) as the reason for rejection. Still, that God responds independently of human deserving is implied elsewhere in the Pentateuch (e.g., Deut. 7:7-8). In any case, Cain responds to the rejection of his offering with anger and disappointment.

> (8) Cain said to his brother Abel, "Let us go out to the field." And when they were in the field, Cain rose up against his brother Abel, and killed him.

Though it was God who had regarded their offerings differently, Cain takes out his anger and disappointment on his brother. Cain lures Abel out into the field and kills him.

> (9) Then the LORD said to Cain, "Where is your brother Abel?" He said, "I do not know; am I my brother's keeper?"

God responds to Cain's behavior as God responded to the behavior of the man and woman in Genesis 3, not with condemnation but with a question. God asked the man and woman, Where are you? God asks Cain, Where is your brother Abel? In neither instance do the human beings answer God's question directly, but here Cain lies. He pretends not to know where Abel is and returns God's question with another question, denying responsibility for his brother's whereabouts and well-being.

These verses establish the rivalry, although the narrative continues. A man determines that God deals more favorably with his brother than with him, and this becomes a source of jealousy and anger. His rage leads to his brother's murder.

### Genesis 25:24-31

> (24) When her [Rebekah's] time to give birth was at hand, there were twins in her womb. (25) The first came out red,

all his body like a hairy mantle; so they named him Esau. (26) Afterward his brother came out, with his hand gripping Esau's heel; so he was named Jacob. Isaac was sixty years old when she bore them.

This announcement of twin sons for Isaac and Rebekah foreshadows their lives. The elder is Esau, though his younger brother Jacob emerges clutching Esau's heel. Jacob will supplant his hairy brother.

(27) When the boys grew up, Esau was a skillful hunter, a man of the field, while Jacob was a quiet man, living in tents. (28) Isaac loved Esau, because he was fond of game; but Rebekah loved Jacob.

The narrator accentuates the brothers' differences: one a hunter, a man of the field; the other quiet, living in tents. One is preferred by his father, the other by his mother.

(29) Once when Jacob was cooking a stew, Esau came in from the field, and he was famished. (30) Esau said to Jacob, "Let me eat some of that red stuff, for I am famished!" (Therefore he was called Edom.) (31) Jacob said, "First sell me your birthright."

The illustration of their differences continues. While Jacob cooks, Esau is hungry. When Esau asks for Jacob's stew, Jacob is willing to give—but only in return for what Esau has. The trade is fair only on the surface: Jacob possesses food, eaten today and gone tomorrow, but Esau's birthright carries long-lasting implications. Jacob takes advantage of Esau's vulnerability—he is famished—by demanding something of considerably greater value than what Jacob will give in exchange. This incident sets the stage for the competition that follows.

### Genesis 27:18-29

(18) So he [Jacob] went in to his father, and said, "My father"; and he [Isaac] said, "Here I am; who are you, my son?" (19) Jacob said to his father, "I am Esau your firstborn.

I have done as you told me; now sit up and eat of my game,
so that you may bless me."

With Isaac close to death he wishes to bless his elder son. Before
bestowing the blessing, however, he asks to eat food that Esau has
prepared. With his mother Rebekah's help, Jacob disguises himself
as Esau and tricks Isaac into believing that he is Esau. He brings
the requested food to his father. Isaac, who is blind, asks whoever
has addressed him to identify himself. Jacob identifies himself as
Esau, tells his father to eat the food he has brought, and then
requests a blessing.

> (20) But Isaac said to his son, "How is it that you have found
> it so quickly, my son?" He answered, "Because the LORD your
> God granted me success."

When Isaac asks how it was possible for Esau to have found and
prepared the food so quickly, Jacob lies again. He attributes his
success to God.

> (21) Then Isaac said to Jacob, "Come near, that I may feel you,
> my son, to know whether you are really my son Esau or not."

Isaac cannot see the man who has brought him food and has
wondered how Esau procured the food so quickly. Now he asks to
use his sense of touch to identify his son.

> (22) So Jacob went up to his father Isaac, who felt him and
> said, "The voice is Jacob's voice, but the hands are the hands
> of Esau." (23) He did not recognize him, because his hands
> were hairy like his brother Esau's hands; so he blessed him.

Isaac, who could not see his son and who wondered how Esau
had procured the food so quickly, has been listening to Jacob's
voice. But when he touches the man's hands, they are—because of
Jacob's deception—hairy like Esau's. The hairy hands deceive the
blind old man into believing that Esau is with him, despite the
voice of Jacob. So he blesses him.

> (24) He said, "Are you really my son Esau?" He answered,
> "I am."

A second opportunity to lie or tell the truth, to cheat his brother or to confess his deceit, presents itself when Isaac asks directly if he is Esau. Jacob says that he is.

> (25) Then he said, "Bring it to me, that I may eat of my son's game and bless you." So he brought it to him, and he ate; and he brought him wine, and he drank.

What could the blind father do? He had spoken his uncertainty, but he had twice been assured that his elder son Esau was indeed speaking with him. Isaac consented to eat the food the man had prepared, and to bless him.

> (26) Then his father Isaac said to him, "Come near and kiss me, my son." (27) So he came near and kissed him; and he smelled the smell of his garments, and blessed him, and said, "Ah, the smell of my son is like the smell of a field that the LORD has blessed."

Does Isaac ask for the kiss because he is still not quite sure if the man is Esau, or is the kiss merely a gesture of intimacy before the blessing? Whatever the reason, Isaac's request allows him to smell Esau's garments, which carry the smell of the field. The scent seems to allay once and for all his fears that he is being deceived, that the voice he hears belongs to Jacob. The deception—Jacob in Esau's clothing—proves successful.

> (28) "May God give you of the dew of heaven, and of the fatness of the earth, and plenty of grain and wine. (29) Let peoples serve you, and nations bow down to you. Be lord over your brothers, and may your mother's sons bow down to you. Cursed be everyone who curses you, and blessed be everyone who blesses you!"

The blessing asks God for fertility that results in prosperity; asks for security, even superiority; and asks that good come to those working toward his son's good, and evil to those perpetrating evil toward his son (cf. Gen. 12:3).

Though the narrative here is condensed, and highlights the encounter between Isaac and Jacob, the reader can anticipate

Esau's anger, for Jacob already had taken his birthright in exchange for food. Now, again, Jacob has given food, this time to his father, and received his father's blessing, intended for Esau, in exchange.

Jacob's deceit, which cheated Esau out of his father's blessing, could only lead to Esau's anger. Jacob flees in fear.

### Genesis 37:4-11

> (4) But when his [Joseph's] brothers saw that their father [Jacob] loved him more than all his brothers, they hated him, and could not speak peaceably to him.

Just as Esau, whom his father loved, was treated badly by Jacob, Jacob's preference for his son Joseph prompts the jealous brothers' ill-treatment of Joseph. They hate him.

> (5) Once Joseph had a dream, and when he told it to his brothers, they hated him even more. (6) He said to them, "Listen to this dream that I dreamed. (7) There we were, binding sheaves in the field. Suddenly my sheaf rose and stood upright; then your sheaves gathered around it, and bowed down to my sheaf."

Joseph's dream positions him above his brothers, which they resent. They despise him.

> (8) His brothers said to him, "Are you indeed to reign over us? Are you indeed to have dominion over us?" So they hated him even more because of his dreams and his words.

Interpreting Joseph's dreams as indicators of his superior status in the future, they hate Joseph even more.

> (9) He had another dream, and told it to his brothers, saying, "Look, I have had another dream: the sun, the moon, and eleven stars were bowing down to me."

Joseph's report of dreams that clearly assert his superior status could only cause already jealous brothers to become more resentful. They could only hate him more.

(10) But when he told it to his father and to his brothers, his
father rebuked him, and said to him, "What kind of dream
is this that you have had? Shall we indeed come, I and your
mother and your brothers, and bow to the ground before
you?" (11) So his brothers were jealous of him, but his
father kept the matter in mind.

As Joseph's first dream led to questions about implications of
his superiority, the second dream prompts similar questions from
his father regarding Joseph's relationships within his family.
Whereas the dreams lead to jealousy in Joseph's brothers, his
father simply tucks the information away for future reference. Any
indication that one sibling is "better" or will fare better than other
siblings, any trace of superiority, breeds jealousy.

# War

### Exodus 17:8-16

(8) Then Amalek came and fought with Israel at Rephidim.

According to the genealogy in Gen. 36:12, Amalek is Esau's
grandson, the son of Esau's son Eliphaz's union with a concubine
named Timna. Such pedigree indicates the unfavorable status of
Amalek and of those, presumably the Amalekites, who fought
with him, thereby tilting the reader's sympathy toward Israel.
Moreover, the wording of the verse places Amalek on the offensive
and Israel on the defensive, also shifting the reader's sympathies
toward Israel. Rephidim is identified as the place of the Israelites'
encampment (Exod. 17:1).

(9) Moses said to Joshua, "Choose some men for us and go
out, fight with Amalek. Tomorrow I will stand on the top of
the hill with the staff of God in my hand."

In the Bible's first reference to Joshua, Moses tells him to function as military leader. He adds that he will be standing on the top
of the hill, holding in his hand the staff of God. The "top of the hill"
is a place of encounter with God. In addition, peoples of the
ancient Near East were known to worship on the high places. The

"staff of God" harkens back to Exod. 4:2, where Moses' staff became the instrument of God's power.

> (10) So Joshua did as Moses told him, and fought with Amalek, while Moses, Aaron, and Hur went up to the top of the hill. (11) Whenever Moses held up his hand, Israel prevailed; and whenever he lowered his hand, Amalek prevailed.

Clearly not only Joshua is engaged in fighting. The act of Moses holding up his hand is indispensably related to his people's success.

> (12) But Moses' hands grew weary; so they took a stone and put it under him, and he sat on it. Aaron and Hur held up his hands, one on one side, and the other on the other side; so his hands were steady until the sun set. (13) And Joshua defeated Amalek and his people with the sword.

The narrative dramatizes the role of Moses' hands in the Israelite victory. When he tires, the two men who have accompanied him provide support, and his hands are held high until the Israelites achieve victory. While Joshua defeats the aggressor with the sword, God is involved through Moses, whose upheld hands may be interpreted as interceding with God.

> (14) Then the LORD said to Moses, "Write this as a reminder in a book and recite it in the hearing of Joshua: I will utterly blot out the remembrance of Amalek from under heaven." (15) And Moses built an altar and called it, The LORD is my banner.

That God had acted previously on Israel's behalf becomes the basis of Israel's confidence that God will protect it in the future. The future will bring Amalek's total defeat. God, through Moses, assures Israel's military leader that he can count on that. Moses, perhaps in the form of a thanksgiving sacrifice, acknowledges God's power and intervention on Israel's behalf. The altar is named after the event (or the perpetual lesson). The Lord as banner announces holy war: "God fights for Israel."

(16) He said, "A hand upon the banner of the LORD! The LORD will have war with Amalek from generation to generation."

The final verses of the literary unit may refer to the staff of God, which Moses probably held in his upheld hands, or to the altar. In either case, "the LORD will have war" over and over again with Amalek. God will fight for Israel.

Of the many passages in the Pentateuch that describe war, this text is particularly disheartening. While Israel is not represented as the aggressor in this passage, by crediting God as warrior and conqueror Israel legitimates and even sacralizes its own domination of others.

## Economics, Competition, and Greed

### Genesis 13:2-7

> (2) Now Abram was very rich in livestock, in silver, and in gold. (3) He journeyed on by stages from the Negeb as far as Bethel, to the place where his tent had been at the beginning, between Bethel and Ai, (4) to the place where he had made an altar at the first; and there Abram called on the name of the LORD.

Verse 2 indicates clearly that the Lord had blessed Abram abundantly. In a culture that did not believe in life after death, God's blessings came in the form of long life, many children to continue one's life after death, and great prosperity. Abram has received great prosperity.

> (5) Now Lot, who went with Abram, also had flocks and herds and tents . . .

Abram's nephew was also blessed by God. One may conclude that he was not blessed as abundantly as Abram, but he too had received God's blessing of prosperity.

... (6) so that the land could not support both of them living together; for their possessions were so great that they could not live together ...

As the result of Abram's and Lot's abundant material possessions, the land could not support them. One concludes that the people, including servants, were so numerous that huge quantities of food were needed to feed them—and huge plots of land needed to grow food. The animals apparently were so numerous that huge fields, in addition to existing fields, were needed for grazing.

... (7a) and there was strife between the herders of Abram's livestock and the herders of Lot's livestock.

When resources are limited, competition results, and in lieu of conservation an impulse to take develops. And when one takes from a limited supply, others needing the resources become resentful, even aggressive. The verse uncovers one of the problems associated with the support and holding of possessions, which is the friction they cause during times of limited supply.

(7b) At that time the Canaanites and the Perizzites lived in the land.

This sentence suggests that the families of Abram and Lot were not the only competitors for the land and its produce. The only solution short of war was to tap new resources, which is why, as the narrative continues, the families of Abram and Lot separate. In this scenario, more land is available. What happens where essential resources are not in unlimited supply?

### Genesis 26:12-22

(12) Isaac sowed seed in that land, and in the same year reaped a hundredfold. The LORD blessed him, (13) and the man became rich; he prospered more and more until he became very wealthy. (14) He had possessions of flocks and herds, and a great household, so that the Philistines envied him. (15) (Now the Philistines had stopped up and filled with earth all the wells that his father's servants had dug in

the days of his father Abraham.) (16) And Abimelech said to Isaac, "Go away from us; you have become too powerful for us."

After a famine had driven Isaac into Gerar, a land ruled by King Abimelech of the Philistines, he and his family settled there. Blessed by the Lord, his land became productive and his livestock and family increased; he became very prosperous. Unfortunately, Isaac's prosperity produced envy among the people with whom he lived as a resident alien and forced Abimelech to expel him. Parenthetically, the narrator reminds his audience that Abraham's servants once had dug wells in Gerar when Abraham was a sojourner there (see Genesis 20).

> (17) So Isaac departed from there and camped in the valley of Gerar and settled there. (18) Isaac dug again the wells of water that had been dug in the days of his father Abraham; for the Philistines had stopped them up after the death of Abraham; and he gave them the names that his father had given them.

Once expelled from Gerar, Isaac's large family as well as his large herds and flocks needed water to survive. Isaac therefore redug the abandoned wells and gave them their earlier names. To the extent that naming is claiming, Isaac claimed his father's wells as his own.

> (19) But when Isaac's servants dug in the valley and found there a well of spring water, (20) the herders of Gerar quarreled with Isaac's herders, saying, "The water is ours." So he called the well Esek, because they contended with him.

Water was a precious resource, essential for the lives of all plants, animals, and human beings, indispensable for preserving Isaac's prosperity and also his very life. Once Isaac has found a well of spring water, the herders of Gerar wish to claim it. Isaac renames the well "contention" because of the conflict over ownership.

(21) Then they dug another well, and they quarreled over
that one also; so he called it Sitnah.

The second reclaimed well is renamed "enmity" because of the
growing animosity between Isaac's people and the herders of
Gerar.

(22) He moved from there and dug another well, and they
did not quarrel over it; so he called it Rehoboth, saying,
"Now the LORD has made room for us, and we shall be fruitful in the land."

Once the herders of Gerar had plenty of water, Isaac and his
family were permitted to use the third well. Isaac renames it
"broad places" or "room," signifying that with room—and with
water—Isaac and his family now could prosper.

The prosperity of others may cause envy, and envy may lead to
aggression and theft from those already perceived as powerful and
who claim the wherewithal to become more powerful. Stakes are
high when two groups compete for limited natural resources.

### Genesis 47:13-26

(13) Now there was no food in all the land, for the famine
was very severe. The land of Egypt and the land of Canaan
languished because of the famine. (14) Joseph collected all
the money to be found in the land of Egypt and in the land
of Canaan, in exchange for the grain that they bought; and
Joseph brought the money into Pharaoh's house. (15) When
the money from the land of Egypt and from the land of
Canaan was spent, all the Egyptians came to Joseph, and
said, "Give us food! Why should we die before your eyes? For
our money is gone."

Supply and demand are keys to economics. As supply diminishes, demand increases. When the people's own food supplies
were exhausted, they bought food from Pharaoh's storehouses.
Eventually, however, they ran out of the money they had been pay-
ing for food. Yet they still needed food.

(16) And Joseph answered, "Give me your livestock, and I will give you food in exchange for your livestock, if your money is gone." (17) So they brought their livestock to Joseph; and Joseph gave them food in exchange for the horses, the flocks, the herds, and the donkeys. That year he supplied them with food in exchange for all their livestock.

Joseph's ability to interpret Pharaoh's dream had allowed him to prepare for the famine. With food stored in warehouses, he could satisfy the people's demand. When they ran out of money, he demanded their animals. People who had had food, money, and animals became people who had food and animals; then they became people who only had food.

(18) When that year was ended, they came to him the following year, and said to him, "We can not hide from my lord that our money is all spent; and the herds of cattle are my lord's. There is nothing left in the sight of my lord but our bodies and our lands. (19) Shall we die before your eyes, both we and our land? Buy us and our land in exchange for food. We with our land will become slaves to Pharaoh; just give us seed, so that we may live and not die, and that the land may not become desolate."

In desperation, with no money or animals to exchange for food, the people implore Joseph to give seed in exchange for their land and themselves. They will work what will now be Pharaoh's land in exchange for a portion of what it yields; at least that will prevent their starvation.

(20) So Joseph bought all the land of Egypt for Pharaoh. All the Egyptians sold their fields, because the famine was severe upon them; and the land became Pharaoh's. (21) As for the people, he made slaves of them from one end of Egypt to the other.

Joseph agreed to the proposition and allowed the people's land to become Pharaoh's and the people themselves to become Pharaoh's slaves.

> (22) Only the land of the priests he did not buy; for the priests had a fixed allowance from Pharaoh, and lived on the allowance that Pharaoh gave them; therefore they did not sell their land.

The only exception to the arrangement was the priest's land, since the priests were entitled to food from the Pharaoh for their services (and perhaps food from sacrifices).

> (23) Then Joseph said to the people, "Now that I have this day bought you and your land for Pharaoh, here is seed for you; sow the land. (24) And at the harvests you shall give one-fifth to Pharaoh, and four-fifths shall be your own, as seed for the field and as food for yourselves and your households, and as food for your little ones."

Joseph required that one-fifth of what the Egyptians produced was to be given to Pharaoh and that the remaining four-fifths could be used for food for their families and for seed.

> (25) They said, "You have saved our lives; may it please my lord, we will be slaves to Pharaoh." (26) So Joseph made it a statute concerning the land of Egypt, and it stands to this day, that Pharaoh should have the fifth. The land of the priests alone did not become Pharaoh's.

According to these provisions, all Egypt would belong to Pharaoh, except the land of the priests. Moreover, both in bountiful harvests and in years of sparse yield, one-fifth of the harvest would belong to Pharaoh.

There are at least two ways of reading the narrative. It is possible to conclude that (1) Joseph and Pharaoh are just, or even generous, in that they require only one-fifth of what the people produced in exchange for providing seed needed to survive, at a time when people lacked the wherewithal to pay, or (2) Joseph's policy on behalf of Pharaoh is greedy, taking advantage of a potentially starving people during a natural disaster. The haves use the famine to gain more at the expense of the have-nots.

# Slavery

### Genesis 37:26-28, 36

> (26) Then Judah said to his brothers, "What profit is it if we kill our brother and conceal his blood? (27) Come, let us sell him to the Ishmaelites, and not lay our hands on him, for he is our brother, our own flesh."

Taking slaves as booty of war or subjecting foreigners to forced labor are common notions of slavery in the ancient Near East. In Genesis 37, Joseph, one of Jacob's sons and the object of sibling rivalry (see above), gains a defender in Judah when his other brothers suggest killing him. The text is usually interpreted as showing Judah's moral superiority (and thus contributing justification for his place as ancestor of David; see Genesis 44, especially 44:33). While such an interpretation is possible, the fact remains that Judah's strategy for swaying his brothers is to persuade them to sell Joseph as a slave. They would receive payment if they sold him; if he were dead, they would receive nothing. Profit becomes the incentive for not killing their brother.

> (28) When some Midianite traders passed by, they drew Joseph up, lifting him out of the pit, and sold him to the Ishmaelites for twenty pieces of silver. And they took Joseph to Egypt.

Most commentaries explain the conflation of the Ishmaelites and the Midianites as the inclusion of two ancient sources. Whatever the reason for the seeming disparity, the differences between the two peoples collapse when it is understood that they both represent enemies of Israel. The Ishmaelites are identified as the descendants of Abraham's son Ishmael, by the Egyptian Hagar, while the Midianites are identified as the descendants of Abraham's son by Keturah. Neither descended from Abraham's chosen son Isaac.

Unfortunately, it is not possible to determine the relative value of the twenty silver pieces as the purchase price for Joseph, though

Exod. 21:32 demands payment of thirty silver pieces if one man's ox gores another man's slave.

> (36) Meanwhile the Midianites had sold him in Egypt to Potiphar, one of Pharaoh's officials, the captain of the guard.

The verse implies further sale and further profit. Sold to the traders for twenty pieces of silver, how much profit did the traders make when they resold Joseph to one of Pharaoh's officials, who is significant enough to be named? The text reduces people to payment and indirectly suggests that cost is determined by the buyer's ability to pay. Human persons are objectified as items of monetary value.

## Water Pollution
### Exodus 7:14-19

> (14) Then the LORD said to Moses, "Pharaoh's heart is hardened; he refuses to let the people go. (15) Go to Pharaoh in the morning, as he is going out to the water; stand by at the river bank to meet him, and take in your hand that staff that was turned into a snake. (16) Say to him, 'The LORD, the God of the Hebrews, sent me to you to say, "Let my people go, so that they may worship me in the wilderness." But until now you have not listened.' (17) Thus says the LORD, "By this you shall know that I am the LORD." See, with the staff that is in my hand I will strike the water that is in the Nile, and it shall be turned to blood. (18) The fish in the river shall die, the river itself shall stink, and the Egyptians shall be unable to drink water from the Nile.'"

The first of the "plagues," or marvelous actions, performed by God on behalf of the Hebrews is to turn the Nile River to blood. Theologians may stress that the incident discloses the power of God to act on behalf of the enslaved people. Historians may ask whether seasonal variations in the mineral content of the clay underlying the water would have made the water appear red and of greater density. But ecologists may take the statement at face value: what once was life-giving is now death-dealing. The Egyptians' most abundant source of water—an element essential to the preservation of life—has become contaminated.

> (19) The LORD said to Moses, "Say to Aaron, 'Take your staff and stretch out your hand over the waters of Egypt—over its rivers, its canals, and its ponds, and all its pools of water—so that they may become blood; and there shall be blood throughout the whole land of Egypt, even in vessels of wood and in vessels of stone.'"

Though the plague is usually associated with the Nile, the text records the pollution of the Egyptians' entire water supply. Unless the effects of the judgment are revoked, the Egyptians are condemned to death. Lack of this natural resource, on which not only human life but all life forms depend, or its contamination, sets in motion an all-embracing ecological imbalance; it is a death sentence.

## Ecological Imbalance

### Exodus 8:2-6, 16-17, 21, 24

> (2) "If you [Pharaoh] refuse to let them go, I will plague your whole country with frogs. (3) The river shall swarm with frogs; they shall come up into your palace, into your bedchamber and your bed, and into the houses of your officials and of your people, and into your ovens and your kneading bowls. (4) The frogs shall come up on you and on your people and on all your officials."

In themselves, frogs are not harmful. They become difficult in disproportionate numbers and when they come indoors, where people sleep and cook, and when they crawl onto people. The plague does not consist of the frogs themselves, but in their number and location.

> (5) And the LORD said to Moses, "Say to Aaron, 'Stretch out your hand with your staff over the rivers, the canals, and the pools, and make frogs come up on the land of Egypt.'"
> (6) So Aaron stretched out his hand over the waters of

Egypt; and the frogs came up and covered the land of
Egypt.

Pharaoh had been warned, but refused to heed the warning.
The frogs that previously had inhabited the waters now invade the
dry and humanly inhabited land.

(16) Then the LORD said to Moses, "Say to Aaron, 'Stretch
out your staff and strike the dust of the earth, so that it may
become gnats throughout the whole land of Egypt.' " (17)
And they did so; Aaron stretched out his hand with his staff
and struck the dust of the earth, and gnats came on humans
and animals alike; all the dust of the earth turned into gnats
throughout the whole land of Egypt.

Pharaoh's refusal to release the Hebrews into the desert is the
occasion for another plague. Gnats in normal supply are not life-
threatening. But the text in describing their superabundance com-
pares them to dust, suggesting that the millions of dust particles
became gnats. The gnats found a resting place on the skin of
humans and other animals. Their excessive numbers, exacerbated
by their location, brought on the ecological imbalance.

(21) For if you will not let my people go, I will send swarms
of flies on you, your officials, and your people, and into your
houses; and the houses of the Egyptians shall be filled with
swarms of flies; so also the land where they live. . . . (24) The
LORD did so, and great swarms of flies came into the house
of Pharaoh and into his officials' houses; and in all of Egypt
the land was ruined because of the flies.

Flies are destructive and carry disease. Swarms depict a species
out of control. Both the increase in population and their location
inside homes constitute a threatening imbalance of nature.

### Exodus 9:2-3, 6, 8-10, 22-25

(2) For if you refuse to let them go and still hold them, (3)
the hand of the LORD will strike with a deadly pestilence
your livestock in the field: the horses, the donkeys, the

camels, the herds, and the flocks. . . . (6) And on the next day the LORD did so; all the livestock of the Egyptians died, but of the livestock of the Israelites not one died.

Though nature finds ways to keep the numbers of a species in check and proportional to the well-being of the environment, a pestilence can disturb the population balance and threaten life forms that depend on the affected species. The animals devastated by the pestilence described in this text are essential to Egyptian travel, food, and commerce. Their decimation would yield disastrous consequences.

> (8) Then the LORD said to Moses and Aaron, "Take handfuls of soot from the kiln, and let Moses throw it in the air in the sight of Pharaoh. (9) It shall become fine dust all over the land of Egypt, and shall cause festering boils on humans and animals throughout the whole land of Egypt." (10) So they took soot from the kiln, and stood before Pharaoh, and Moses threw it in the air, and it caused festering boils on humans and animals.

Though not described here as life-threatening, hot soot can nevertheless cause painful burns. Skin sores are easily prone to infection; infections not properly attended can eventually cause death. The text describes an unnatural occurrence—not burns by accident, or burns affecting a few, but festering boils affecting all the Egyptians and their animals. Surely such a situation represents nature out of control.

> (22) The LORD said to Moses, "Stretch out your hand toward heaven so that hail may fall on the whole land of Egypt, on humans and animals and all the plants of the field in the land of Egypt." (23) Then Moses stretched out his staff toward heaven, and the LORD sent thunder and hail, and fire came down on the earth. And the LORD rained hail on the land of Egypt; (24) there was hail with fire flashing continually in the midst of it, such heavy hail as had never fallen in all the land of Egypt since it became a nation. (25) The hail struck down everything that was in the open field

throughout all the land of Egypt, both human and animal; the hail also struck down all the plants of the field, and shattered every tree in the field.

The amount and size of the hail and the extent of land on which the hail fell—these factors make for an unusual, and deadly, situation. Excess destroys.

### Exodus 10:4-6, 13-15

(4) "For if you refuse to let my people go, tomorrow I will bring locusts into your country. (5) They shall cover the surface of the land, so that no one will be able to see the land. They shall devour the last remnant left you after the hail, and they shall devour every tree of yours that grows in the field. (6) They shall fill your houses, and the houses of all your officials and of all the Egyptians—something that neither your parents nor your grandparents have seen, from the day they came on earth to this day." Then he turned and went out from Pharaoh.

. . . (13) So Moses stretched out his staff over the land of Egypt, and the LORD brought an east wind upon the land all that day and all that night; when morning came, the east wind had brought the locusts. (14) The locusts came upon all the land of Egypt and settled on the whole country of Egypt, such a dense swarm of locusts as had never been before, nor ever shall be again. (15) They covered the surface of the whole land, so that the land was black; and they ate all the plants in the land and all the fruit of the trees that the hail had left; nothing green was left, no tree, no plant in the field, in all the land of Egypt.

The plague of locusts proves more deadly than the natural disasters preceding it. Their excessive number is conveyed by stating that they overcame the land, which was black with them. They infested the houses of Egyptian people, great and small alike, and wiped out the remnant from the hailstorm. They ate the plants, anything green that was left. If they destroyed everything green, what would the animals eat? What would the Egyptians eat? If there was nothing to eat, how would they survive?

Traditionally described as miracles, these unusual natural disasters assert the power of the Hebrews' God over the forces of nature; described as plagues, the negative character of the disasters is underscored. Whether these events actually happened as described is not at issue here. Rather, the text points to the authors' belief in God's power over creation, their awareness of human dependence on nature, and the potential for cosmological harm if the elements of creation get out of balance. The authors understand well the ripple effect of excess or lack—lack of drinking water and of plant and animal life or excess of frogs, gnats, flies, hail, and locusts.

# Part Three

# 6

# Liberation

## Courageous Midwives

### Exodus 1:15-21

> (15) The king of Egypt said to the Hebrew midwives, one of whom was named Shiphrah and the other Puah, (16) "When you act as midwives to the Hebrew women, and see them on the birthstool, if it is a boy, kill him; but if it is a girl, she shall live." (17) But the midwives feared God; they did not do as the king of Egypt commanded them, but they let the boys live.

The identification of the Hebrew midwives by name—Shiphrah and Puah—suggests their significance in Israelite culture. Fertility was seen as a blessing from God; those who facilitated fertility had a responsibility to the larger society, most likely acknowledged by allotting them a degree of status.

The king of Egypt orders the women, who, although midwives with status among their own people, were still subject to the king, to kill all the male infants born to Hebrew women, but to allow the females to live. Because males in patriarchal societies are of more value than females, the male offspring were seen as more of a threat to their Egyptian overlords. The female infants, in contrast, represented a valuable source of concubinage and other work. As the text juxtaposes male and female infants, it also juxtaposes the authority of God and Pharaoh. Pharaoh orders the midwives, but, obeying God, they disregard the orders of the king. Risky business!

> (18) So the king of Egypt summoned the midwives and said to them, "Why have you done this, and allowed the boys to live?" (19) The midwives said to Pharaoh, "Because the Hebrew women are not like the Egyptian women; for they are vigorous and give birth before the midwife comes to them."

The male Hebrew infants are not being killed and Pharaoh's command is being ignored. Summoning the women, he demands an account. The midwives contrast Hebrew and Egyptian women, explaining that, whereas the Egyptian women do not give birth until the arrival of the midwives, the labor of the Hebrew women is short. The child thus is born before the midwife's arrival. A contemporary consciousness is often tempted to accuse the midwives of lying, but in reality their actions affirmed life; the midwives, who "feared God," merely tricked a death-dealing king.

> (20) So God dealt well with the midwives; and the people multiplied and became very strong.

God blesses faithfulness, and the midwives, acting on behalf of their people, have been faithful. Blessings usually occur in the form of long life, many children, and prosperity. God blessed the people with progeny.

> (21) And because the midwives feared God, he gave them families.

God was understood to be the One responsible for opening all wombs, and, for women, the greatest blessing was to become the mother of children. The midwives who had "feared God" and behaved accordingly—at unknown personal risk—are indeed blessed. They who had preserved the lives of Hebrew males themselves receive "houses" or "households." Within a narrative showing that life is stronger than death, the midwives choose life (see also Deut. 30:11-20).

# A Burning Bush, a Sacred Mountain

### Exodus 3:1-12

> (1) Moses was keeping the flock of his father-in-law Jethro, the priest of Midian; he led his flock beyond the wilderness, and came to Horeb, the mountain of God. (2) There the angel of the LORD appeared to him in a flame of fire out of a bush; he looked, and the bush was blazing, yet it was not consumed.

Verses 1-2 set the scene. Moses had fled from Egypt and settled among the Midianites, marrying Zipporah, the daughter of the priest of Midian (Exod. 2:15-22). Working as a shepherd he led his sheep to Mount Horeb. The narrator identifies this mountain as sacred to God, perhaps because of the event he is about to relate. A messenger from God appears in a "flame of fire" (God's glory appears as a devouring fire in Exod. 24:13). The extraordinary character of the fire is underlined: the bush burns but the fire does not consume it.

> (3) Then Moses said, "I must turn aside and look at this great sight, and see why the bush is not burned up." (4) When the LORD saw that he had turned aside to see, God called to him out of the bush, "Moses, Moses!" And he said, "Here I am."

An extraordinary sight catches Moses' attention, and he draws close to examine it. God addresses Moses by name from the bush; Moses acknowledges the call.

> (5) Then he said, "Come no closer! Remove the sandals from your feet, for the place on which you are standing is holy ground." (6) He said further, "I am the God of your father, the God of Abraham, the God of Isaac, and the God of Jacob." And Moses hid his face, for he was afraid to look at God.

The flame of fire that was not consumed is associated with holiness, otherness, and separation. Moses is to remain at a distance and to remove his sandals, both appropriate gestures when in the presence of the God of Moses' ancestors. Moses' spontaneous response is to turn his face away (see also Num. 4:20).

> (7) Then the LORD said, "I have observed the misery of my people who are in Egypt; I have heard their cry on account of their taskmasters. Indeed, I know their sufferings, (8) and I have come down to deliver them from the Egyptians, and to bring them up out of that land to a good and broad land, a land flowing with milk and honey, to the country of the Canaanites, the Hittites, the Amorites, the Perizzites, the Hivites, and the Jebusites. (9) The cry of the Israelites has now come to me; I have also seen how the Egyptians oppress them. (10) So come, I will send you to Pharaoh to bring my people, the Israelites, out of Egypt."

Having called Moses using fire that does not consume, God sends him to Pharaoh to deliver the people from their sufferings. Moses is sent to deliver the people to a good and broad land, a land where others live but which is described as extraordinarily fruitful.

> (11) But Moses said to God, "Who am I that I should go to Pharaoh, and bring the Israelites out of Egypt?" (12) He said, "I will be with you; and this shall be the sign for you that it is I who sent you: when you have brought the people out of Egypt, you shall worship God on this mountain."

Moses' question reveals his hesitation and is quickly answered, though indirectly. Who am I? Moses asks. Moses is the one whom God will accompany, and when Moses has succeeded in his task he will return to the very place he now stands on the mountain and worship God.

Fire, a bush, abundant "milk and honey," and a mountain— these gifts of nature all help effect the call of Moses and facilitate the people's deliverance from bondage.

# Liberating Water

### Exodus 14:15-16, 21-23, 26-29

(15) The LORD said to Moses, "Why do you cry out to me? Tell the Israelites to go forward. (16) But you lift up your staff, and stretch out your hand over the sea and divide it, that the Israelites may go into the sea on dry ground."

Advancing Egyptians trap the Israelites at the sea. What can they do? God quickly silences Moses' concern with a directive to advance. Moses is ordered to lift up his staff (cf. Exod. 4:3-5) and to extend his hand over the sea, a gesture that will divide the sea and expose dry land. The Israelites will be able to cross between the divided sea.

(21) Then Moses stretched out his hand over the sea. The LORD drove the sea back by a strong east wind all night, and turned the sea into dry land; and the waters were divided. (22) The Israelites went into the sea on dry ground, the waters forming a wall for them on their right and on their left.

Moses obeyed the Lord's word and extended his hand over the sea. With a strong east wind, the Lord drove the sea back so the dry land could appear. Pushed by the wind, the water formed walls on the north and south sides, making it possible for the Israelites to move toward the sea on dry land.

(23) The Egyptians pursued, and went into the sea after them, all of Pharaoh's horses, chariots, and chariot drivers.

The Egyptians continued their pursuit on dry ground.

(26) Then the LORD said to Moses, "Stretch out your hand over the sea, so that the water may come back upon the Egyptians, upon their chariots and chariot drivers."

The Lord commands Moses again to stretch his hand out over the sea; this time, however, instead of an east wind parting the water, the water would come together and cover the pursuing Egyptians.

> (27) So Moses stretched out his hand over the sea, and at dawn the sea returned to its normal depth. As the Egyptians fled before it, the LORD tossed the Egyptians into the sea. (28) The waters returned and covered the chariots and the chariot drivers, the entire army of Pharaoh that had followed them into the sea; not one of them remained.

Moses obeyed the Lord's command. Whereas the sea had parted during the night, at dawn the waters came together. The scrambling Egyptians tried to run but were unsuccessful, and they all drowned.

> (29) But the Israelites walked on dry ground through the sea, the waters forming a wall for them on their right and on their left.

All the Israelites escaped, delivered from bondage in Egypt and from the pursuing Egyptians. The water became for them liberating water, having facilitated their escape and destroyed their enemy.

## Manna and Quail
### Exodus 16:4a, 12-15, 31-32

> (4a) Then the LORD said to Moses, "I am going to rain bread from heaven for you, and each day the people shall go out and gather enough for that day."

Liberation from Egypt was only the first step in the people's journey to a land promised to their ancestors. To arrive at their destination, they had to traverse a wilderness. To survive the wilderness they needed food. The people complained that they had survived Egypt only to die of hunger in the desert, but the narrative describes how the liberating God would sustain them—with bread, gathered and eaten each day.

(12) "I have heard the complaining of the Israelites; say to them, 'At twilight you shall eat meat, and in the morning you shall have your fill of bread; then you shall know that I am the LORD your God.'"

The people receive more than bread. They will eat bread in the morning and meat in the evening. God's provision for their needs was meant to strengthen faith that God *could* and *would* act on their behalf.

(13) In the evening quails came up and covered the camp; and in the morning there was a layer of dew around the camp. (14) When the layer of dew lifted, there on the surface of the wilderness was a fine flaky substance, as fine as frost on the ground. (15) When the Israelites saw it, they said to one another, "What is it?" For they did not know what it was. Moses said to them, "It is the bread that the LORD has given you to eat."

The Lord kept the promise. Quails provided meat each evening while the "fine flaky substance" on the surface of the wilderness each morning provided bread.

(31) The house of Israel called it manna; it was like coriander seed, white, and the taste of it was like wafers made with honey. (32) Moses said, "This is what the LORD has commanded, 'Let an omer of it be kept throughout your generations, in order that they may see the food with which I fed you in the wilderness, when I brought you out of the land of Egypt.'"

The Lord, through Moses, directs the people to preserve an omer of manna so that future generations could see how the Lord had sustained them after delivering them from Egypt. The preserved manna would function as a permanent reminder of the Lord's saving acts of deliverance. Food is essential for human survival, more essential even than deliverance from bondage.

# Returning to Family and Property

*Leviticus 25:10-13*

> (10) And you shall hallow the fiftieth year and you shall pro-
> claim liberty throughout the land to all its inhabitants. It
> shall be a jubilee for you: you shall return, every one of you,
> to your property and every one of you to your family.

The Jubilee Year, or the fiftieth year, provided for the return of
the land to its original owners, the family who, ideally, never
should have been alienated in the first place. The attachment to
land is illustrated by Zelophehad's daughters, who were required
to marry within their father's tribe to keep hold of the tribe's land
(Num. 36:7); and by Naboth, who could not turn over familial
land, even to a king (1 Kings 21:3). But if Israelites had been
estranged from familial land, returning would allow them to be
reunited with ancestors buried there. The redistribution of land
implies a redistribution of human power relationships.

> (11) That fiftieth year shall be a jubilee for you: you shall not
> sow, or reap the aftergrowth, or harvest the unpruned vines.
> (12) For it is a jubilee; it shall be holy to you: you shall eat
> only what the field itself produces.

During the year of Jubilee even the land was to experience liberation. Farmers were to refrain from sowing new seed, or from
reaping what had grown since the last harvest, or from harvesting
vines that had not been pruned. Unnatural human intervention
was not permitted. All the earth would experience freedom from
actions that might be detrimental to the earth while advancing
others' welfare.

> (13) In this year of jubilee you shall return, everyone of you,
> to your property.

Any land alienated from a particular family because of drought,
famine, sickness, and so forth would return to its original owner;
that is, a family could return to its land. Those who had become
indebted during the previous fifty years would experience eco-

nomic liberation in being reunited with their property and regaining the economic security it provided.

The provisions of the Jubilee Year sought to guarantee equitable relationships among people. The inequality in land distribution (and the consequent potential for prosperity and indebtedness) was not to continue indefinitely. The haves could not use new acquisitions to acquire more, placing the have-nots at a permanent disadvantage (for a contrast, see above, "Economics, Competition, and Greed").

## Returning to God

### Deuteronomy 4:25-31

> (25) When you have had children and children's children, and become complacent in the land, if you act corruptly by making an idol in the form of anything, thus doing what is evil in the sight of the LORD your God, and provoking him to anger, (26) I call heaven and earth to witness against you today that you will soon utterly perish from the land that you are crossing the Jordan to occupy; you will not live long on it, but will be utterly destroyed. (27) The LORD will scatter you among the peoples; only a few of you will be left among the nations where the LORD will lead you. (28) There you will serve other gods made by human hands, objects of wood and stone that neither see, nor hear, nor eat, nor smell.

Moses warns the Israelites, once entering the promised land, not to become complacent regarding their covenant relationship. The Lord's anger will be provoked if they make and worship idols, he says, and swears to the consequences of their idolatry: (1) loss of land; (2) exile; (3) limited survivors; and (4) worship of idols, gods made by human beings.

> (29) From there you will seek the LORD your God, and you will find him if you search after him with all your heart and soul.

Moses' prediction, though dire, is not without hope. From exile the Israelites will seek their God. If they search with wholehearted conviction, they will find God.

> (30) In your distress when all these things have happened to you in time to come, you will return to the LORD your God and heed him.

Moses predicts the exiled people's return to God and renewed loyalty.

> (31) Because the LORD your God is a merciful God, he will neither abandon you nor destroy you; he will not forget the covenant with your ancestors that he swore to them.

God responds when the people return to God with faithfulness. A merciful God does not meet idolatry with abandonment or destruction; rather, God is mindful of the covenant. God is and will remain their God, and they are and will remain God's people.

# 7

# Belonging: Covenantal Relationship

## Circumcision

### *Genesis 17:7-14*

> (7) "I [God] will establish my covenant between me and you, and your offspring after you throughout their generations; for an everlasting covenant, to be God to you and to your offspring after you. (8) And I will give to you, and to your offspring after you, the land where you are now an alien, all the land of Canaan, for a perpetual holding; and I will be their God."

The covenant relationship God establishes with Abraham and his descendants is to be a lasting one. God promises to be the God of Abraham and his descendants. As an expression of this relationship God promises to give Abraham and his descendants the land on which they now dwell as foreigners, the land of Canaan. The land is not the covenant; the covenant is the relationship, the bond, that God establishes with the family of Abraham.

> (9) God said to Abraham, "As for you, you shall keep my covenant, you and your offspring after you throughout their generations."

Keeping covenant refers to attitudes and behaviors that are consistent with the relationship. God directs that Abraham and his descendants respond to the God who has claimed them.

> (10) "This is my covenant, which you shall keep, between me and you and your offspring after you: Every male among you shall be circumcised. (11) You shall circumcise the flesh of your foreskins, and it shall be a sign of the covenant between me and you."

God is explicit about behavior that will signify the people's acceptance of the covenant relationship. They are to ratify the covenant by the act of male circumcision. Though this is also an expression of patriarchy—only males can be circumcised—it is an intimate, lasting, and visible sign of being bound to God.

> (12) "Throughout your generations every male among you shall be circumcised when he is eight days old, including the slave born in your house and the one bought with your money from any foreigner who is not of your offspring. (13) Both the slave born in your house and the one bought with your money shall be circumcised. So shall my covenant be in your flesh an everlasting covenant."

The text calls for repeating the act on all males shortly after birth and on all male slaves purchased from foreigners. Just as God has entered into lasting covenant with Abraham to be his God and the God of his descendents, so Abraham's descendents—all the males—are to renew their acceptance of the covenant relationship by the circumcision of the flesh of their foreskins.

> (14) "Any uncircumcised male who is not circumcised in the flesh of his foreskin shall be cut off from his people; he has broken my covenant."

Because God commands circumcision as the sign of the people's acceptance of their covenant relationship, failure to circumcise their boys would result in alienation from the covenant, for the covenant terms would have been violated.

Belonging to the people of God demands a lifetime commitment; the expression of commitment is cut irrevocably into the organ associated with both human fertility and human sensation. The people were to be intimately and irreversibly God's.

### Deuteronomy 10:14-16

> (14) Although heaven and the heaven of heavens belong to the LORD your God, the earth with all that is in it, (15) yet the LORD set his heart in love on your ancestors alone and chose you, their descendants after them, out of all the peoples, as it is today. (16) Circumcise, then, the foreskin of your heart, and do not be stubborn any longer.

Moses' farewell speech to the Israelites includes the assertion that everything belongs to God. Yet Moses assures the Israelites that God has chosen them—ancestors and descendants as well as those in Moses' hearing—to receive God's special love. These assertions form the rationale for exhorting the people to open their hearts fully, making themselves vulnerable, to God. The cutting of male foreskins in circumcision is here made symbolic; everyone can be included. The protective covering over the delicate heart is to be removed so that the heart can be deeply penetrated by God's love.

### Deuteronomy 30:6

> Moreover, the LORD your God will circumcise your heart and the heart of your descendants, so that you will love the LORD your God with all your heart and with all your soul, in order that you may live.

This verse attributes the circumcision of the human heart to God's action. The purpose of circumcision is to enable the people to love the Lord fully; such wholehearted covenant response will issue in the life of the people. God again will act in the people's best interest.

## Covenant: Remembrance, Reading, Renewal

### Exodus 6:2-5

> (2) God also spoke to Moses and said to him, "I am the LORD. (3) I appeared to Abraham, Isaac, and Jacob as God

Almighty, but by my name 'The LORD' I did not make myself known to them."

Names bear great significance in the ancient Near East. For example, God changes the names of Abram and Sarai; Isaac is so named because of Sarah's laughter; and Jacob changes the name of Rachel's son Benoni to Benjamin. In Exodus 3, God's revelation to Moses includes the name "Yahweh," here translated "The LORD." Though patriarchs had called on the name of the Lord (e.g., Gen. 12:8), the context here suggests that God's relationship with the people of the Exodus is even more intimate than it was with the patriarchs.

> (4) I also established my covenant with them, to give them the land of Canaan, the land in which they resided as aliens. (5) I have also heard the groaning of the Israelites whom the Egyptians are holding as slaves, and I have remembered my covenant.

God recalls the covenant with the ancestors of Israel—and the promise to give them the land of Canaan—and also attests knowledge of the people's sufferings in Egypt. That God is even more closely bound to the people after the self-revelation involved in naming, that God recalls the covenant promise of land, and that God now hears the people's cry predict God's future activity on the people's behalf.

### Exodus 24:7-8

> (7) Then he took the book of the covenant, and read it in the hearing of the people; and they said, "All that the LORD has spoken we will do, and we will be obedient." (8) Moses took the blood and dashed it on the people, and said, "See the blood of the covenant that the LORD has made with you in accordance with all these words."

The words inscribed in the book of the covenant attest to God's relationship with the people: the Lord is their god; they are God's people. They have experienced God's action on their behalf and are to respond to the covenant with action consistent with their god's directives, in accordance with covenant teachings.

This covenant renewal ceremony incorporates burnt offerings and offerings of well-being. Moses divides the blood of the sacrifice, dashing one part onto the altar. In order to ratify the covenant and to confirm the people's assent to it, Moses takes the other half of the blood and dashes it onto the people. Both the Lord and the people thereby recommit themselves to the covenant relationship.

## An Obedient Kingdom of Priests

*Exodus 19:5-6*

> (5) Now therefore, if you obey my [God's] voice, and keep my covenant, you shall be my treasured possession out of all the peoples. Indeed, the whole earth is mine, (6) but you shall be for me a priestly kingdom and a holy [people]. These are the words that you [Moses] shall speak to the Israelites.

God recommits in this text to the people of Israel. They will be special to God, a treasured possession among all the peoples of the earth. Reiterating, God tells Moses that he is to inform the people that everything—all the earth—belongs to God and that the people of Israel are to have a special relationship to God. Moreover, their relationship with God creates for the covenant people a special relationship with other peoples, as a priestly kingdom and a holy people. As priests in their society function as mediators between people and God, so the Israelites are to stand between God and other peoples; as holiness separates from the common and ordinary, so the people of Israel are to be separate and distinct.

## The Sabbath

*Exodus 31:12-17*

> (12) The LORD said to Moses: (13) You yourself are to speak to the Israelites: "You shall keep my sabbaths, for this is a sign between me and you throughout your generations, given in order that you may know that I, the LORD, sanctify you."

The historical development of the sabbath may be long and complicated, yet as presented here and elsewhere in many Pentateuchal texts the sabbath occurs on the seventh day of the week as a sign that God rested and was refreshed after the work of creation (Gen. 2:2). Similarly, the Lord's people are to rest on the seventh day, recalling God's creation (Exod. 20:11), and to allow themselves, their families, their male and female slaves, and all their animals to rest (Deut. 5:14). In this text the sabbath is identified as a sign of God's covenant relationship; the people are to keep the sabbath to recognize God as the One who makes them holy.

> (14) "You shall keep the sabbath, because it is holy for you; everyone who profanes it shall be put to death; whoever does any work on it shall be cut off from among the people."

The sabbath here is identified explicitly with the covenant. The sabbath is holy and God's people are to observe it. The importance of observing the sabbath is connected integrally to the covenant relationship itself. God is holy; therefore, the day separated from the others and set aside for God is holy. Anyone who does not keep the sabbath shall be punished. The suggested punishments vary from death to excommunication, but their severity expresses the seriousness of the violation and, conversely, the importance of observing the teaching. To profane the sabbath is to defile the holy; for this reason, the violator deserves death. To work on the sabbath is to debase it, and for debasing it one deserves to be expelled from the covenant people. Such severe punishments express the gravity of the offense, which is rejection of the covenant relationship with God.

> (15) "Six days shall work be done, but the seventh day is a sabbath of solemn rest, holy to the LORD; whoever does any work on the sabbath day shall be put to death."

The text, by way of reiteration, contrasts the six days of work with the solemn day of no work. Serious consequences for violation again are emphasized, the punishment of death again prescribed. There is no greater punishment, illustrating that this violation is of the greatest magnitude.

> (16) "Therefore the Israelites shall keep the sabbath, observing the sabbath throughout their generations, as a perpetual covenant. (17) It is a sign forever between me and the people of Israel that in six days the LORD made heaven and earth, and on the seventh day he rested, and was refreshed."

As with circumcision (see above), the Israelites understood the sabbath as a sign of the covenant relationship. Sabbath observance was to continue perpetually, from one generation to another, just as God's covenant would last through the generations. Sabbath rest was fitting for God's creation, for God had rested from the work of creating on the sabbath.

## Forgiveness and Reconciliation

### Leviticus 26:40-45

> (40) But if they confess their iniquity and the iniquity of their ancestors, in that they committed treachery against me and, moreover, that they continued hostile to me—(41) so that I, in turn, continued hostile to them and brought them into the land of their enemies; if then their uncircumcised heart is humbled and they make amends for their iniquity, (42) then will I remember my covenant with Jacob; I will remember also my covenant with Isaac and also my covenant with Abraham, and I will remember the land.

Infidelity to the covenant relationship with God—once the Israelites have committed to fidelity—will result in punishment. The Israelites would be expelled from the land the Lord had promised (Genesis 12), the land to which Moses had brought them (Deut. 32:52).

But infidelity, even unfaithfulness causing expulsion from the land, would not sever the covenant relationship totally. Acknowledging their unfaithfulness as well as the unfaithfulness of their ancestors, and admitting their refusal to circumcise their hearts (see "Circumcision" above), would prompt the Lord to remember the "good old days" when the Israelites had been faithful. God would remember the covenants made with Abraham, Isaac, and Jacob and God's promise to give them the land.

(43) For the land shall be deserted by them, and enjoy its sabbath years by lying desolate without them, while they shall make amends for their iniquity, because they dared to spurn my ordinances, and they abhorred my statutes.

Oddly enough, the Israelites' punishment in exile meant sabbath rest for the land. As depicted here, the land lay desolate and enjoyed rest while the Israelites were punished for iniquities against their covenant partner. They had reneged on the covenant and had suffered the consequences of infidelity.

(44) Yet for all that, when they are in the land of their enemies, I will not spurn them, or abhor them so as to destroy them utterly and break my covenant with them; for I am the LORD their God; . . .

The iniquities of the Israelites would result in punishment, yes; in their annihilation, never. The Lord their God does punish iniquity—even to the fourth generation—but God does not utterly cast off the people. As depicted in verse 44, the people break the covenant, but God does not. A twofold reason is provided for the discrepancy in behavior between the covenant partners: (1) God is God and, implicitly, more forgiving than humans, and (2) God is God of the Israelites, a faithful covenant partner even in the face of infidelity.

. . . (45) but I will remember in their favor the covenant with their ancestors whom I brought out of the land of Egypt in the sight of the nations, to be their God: I am the LORD.

Memories of God's covenant relationship with the Israelites' ancestors, not only with the patriarchs but also with Moses and the people of the Exodus, inspire God to continue as the people's God, to continue to act in their best interest. While others might reject unfaithful covenant partners or punish them more fully, God will not: God is the Lord.

### Deuteronomy 30:1-5

(1) When all these things have happened to you, the blessings and the curses that I have set before you, if you call

them to mind among all the nations where the LORD your God has driven you, (2) and return to the LORD your God, and you and your children obey him with all your heart and with all your soul, just as I am commanding you today, (3) then the LORD your God will restore your fortunes and have compassion on you, gathering you again from all the peoples among whom the LORD your God has scattered you.

This passage, probably written during Israel's exile, "predicts" the people's unfaithfulness and God's punishment. Nevertheless, God will return abundantly if the people again show faithfulness toward God. God again will act with compassion, will return them to well-being, and even restore them to the land.

(4) Even if you are exiled to the ends of the world, from there the LORD your God will gather you, and from there he will bring you back. (5) The LORD your God will bring you into the land that your ancestors possessed, and you will possess it; he will make you more prosperous and numerous than your ancestors.

No matter how far from their "center of gravity" the people stray, if they return to God, the Lord will return to them. The Lord's return will enable them to return to their land and even to thrive again, to become more prosperous than their ancestors. The restoration is described as undeservedly generous.

## For the Future Also

### Deuteronomy 29:10-15

(10) You stand assembled today, all of you, before the LORD your God—the leaders of your tribes, your elders, and your officials, all the men of Israel, (11) your children, your women, and the aliens who are in your camp, both those who cut your wood and those who draw your water—(12) to enter into the covenant of the LORD your God, sworn by an oath, which the LORD your God is making with you today; . . .

The description includes everyone, from the greatest to the least. Although the enumeration is hierarchical—leaders of tribes, elders, officials, Israelite men, children, women, and resident aliens named in that order—it embraces everyone. The Lord is swearing a covenant with everyone; no one is excluded.

> ... (13) in order that he may establish you today as his people, and that he may be your God, as he promised you and as he swore to your ancestors, to Abraham, to Isaac, and to Jacob.

The covenant consists of the relationship established. God promises to be God for the people while the people promise to be the people of God. "I am your God; you are my people" is the phrase that most succinctly articulates the covenant relationship. God continues to be faithful to the covenant made with Israel's ancestors.

> (14) I am making this covenant, sworn by an oath, not only with you who stand here with us today before the LORD our God, (15) but also with those who are not here with us today.

God remembers the covenant with Israel's ancestors, with Abraham, Isaac, and Jacob. God now makes a covenant with all the assembled—with everyone, with no one excluded. The group now, in the present, becomes God's people, and God becomes their God. But past and present are not enough. God also commits to faithfulness in the future, both in the futures of those present and for future people. God's faithfulness is for yesterday, today, and for a long while to come (literal translation of Hebrew "forever").

# 8

# Reciprocity

## Loving

### God for Persons

*Deuteronomy 4:37*

> And because he [God] loved your ancestors, he chose their
> descendants after them. He brought you out of Egypt with
> his own presence, by his great power.

This verse expresses succinctly both God's love for Israel's ancestors and God's consequent love for their descendants. That love expressed itself in three ways: (1) God delivered the Israelites from Egypt, from bondage and slavery; (2) God was present to the Israelite people; and (3) God used divine power on the people's behalf. Though the verse intricately connects these expressions of God's love, each aspect recurs over and over again as the Israelites narrate their "story" of God's love in its countless expressions for them.

### Persons for God

*Deuteronomy 6:5*

> You shall love the LORD your God with all your heart, and
> with all your soul, and with all your might.

Love is not understood here as sentimental piety but is expressed in covenant fidelity. The text directs the Israelites to the fullness of covenant faithfulness, total obedience to the teachings.

### Deuteronomy 10:12

> So now, O Israel, what does the LORD your God require of you? Only to fear the LORD your God, to walk in all his ways, to love him, to serve the LORD your God with all your heart and with all your soul.

Though this verse resembles a passage often quoted from the prophet Micah, it is embedded here in Moses' teaching. Covenant fidelity consists in taking God seriously—to "fear" God is to hold God in awe, to take the covenant seriously, to assent wholeheartedly to the teachings of God, and to behave in a manner consistent with God's teachings. The people are to respond to God with total conviction.

### Persons for One Another

### Leviticus 19:18

> You shall not take vengeance or bear a grudge against any of your people, but you shall love your neighbor as yourself: I am the LORD.

Among the teachings regarding covenant faithfulness is the directive to refrain from revenge in deed and even from bad feelings toward another. In contrast to such behaviors that divide community, the Israelites are told to maintain the same regard for their neighbors as they do for themselves. The authority behind this directive is identified explicitly as God.

### Leviticus 19:34

> The alien who resides with you shall be to you as the citizen among you; you shall love the alien as yourself, for you were aliens in the land of Egypt: I am the LORD your God.

The text directs the Israelites not to make hierarchical distinctions between citizens and resident aliens, but to regard and treat both groups identically. Not only are Israelites directed to love fellow Israelites, they are directed to love outsiders—resident aliens. The rationale is clear. The Israelites know what it is to be an outsider and to be persecuted. These memories of Egypt should influence their treatment of others.

### Showing Covenant Ḥesed

#### Exodus 15:13

> "In your steadfast love you led the people whom you redeemed; you guided them by your strength to your holy abode."

Miriam and Moses' thanksgiving song for the Lord's deliverance from Egypt includes this assertion: God's covenant faithfulness (*hesed*), translated as "steadfast love," led to the people's redemption; God's strength guided the people to the Lord's dwelling.

#### Exodus 34:6-7a

> (6) The LORD passed before him [Moses] and proclaimed, "The LORD, the LORD, a God merciful and gracious, slow to anger, and abounding in steadfast love and faithfulness, (7a) keeping steadfast love for the thousandth generation, forgiving iniquity and transgression and sin, yet by no means clearing the guilty . . ."

Moses, recalling events on Mount Sinai, reports the second transmission of the Lord's teaching. Moses experiences God's self-revelation on the mountain, that God is merciful, gracious, and slow to anger. Though valuable attributes, given what was to become Israel's history, they pale before the assurance that God abounds in covenant loyalty and faithfulness, that, in fact, God keeps steadfast love even to the thousandth generation.

### Numbers 14:18a, 19

(18a) "The LORD is slow to anger, and abounding in steadfast love, forgiving iniquity and transgression, but by no means clearing the guilty. . . ." (19) Forgive the iniquity of this people according to the greatness of your steadfast love, just as you have pardoned this people, from Egypt even until now.

Moses, after sending messengers to spy on Canaan, reminds the Lord of the Lord's self-revelation. The spies have returned with reports of the enemy's strength, intimidating the Israelites who murmur against the Lord. God's anger prompts Moses to intercede with reminders that God abounds in covenant loyalty and that God forgives transgressions. Based on the Lord's past forgiveness, Moses asks God, in proportion to God's covenant faithfulness, to forgive the most recent behavior.

### Deuteronomy 7:9

Know therefore that the LORD your God is God, the faithful God who maintains covenant loyalty with those who love him and keep his commandments, to a thousand generations.

Who is Israel's God? The Lord is Israel's God. But how can one characterize Israel's God? Israel's God remains faithful to the covenant relationship and maintains steadfast love with those who conform to their own covenant identity, with those who love God and who take God's teachings seriously—now and long into the future.

### Exodus 24:3

Moses came and told the people all the words of the LORD and all the ordinances; and all the people answered with one voice, and said, "All the words that the LORD has spoken we will do."

According to the Bible, God behaves with steadfast love far more often than the people. God's covenant loyalty far excelled the people's. Nevertheless, at times the people affirmed their loyalty. Exod. 24:3 reflects one instance of God's covenant partner Israel professing allegiance. Presented with God's teachings, the people affirm the covenant and their choice to conform.

# Making and Being Holy

## Making Plant, Animal, and Human Sacred

### Exodus 22:29-30

> (29) You shall not delay to make offerings from the fullness of your harvest and from the outflow of your presses.
>
> The firstborn of your sons you shall give to me. (30) You shall do the same with your oxen and your sheep: seven days it shall remain with its mother; on the eighth day you shall give it to me.

Recognizing God as the One responsible for creation and as the One to whom everything ultimately belongs, the peoples of ancient Israel were to act out this belief by offering God the first fruits of their harvest, their firstborn sons, and the firstlings of their herds and flocks. The gesture, acknowledging that everything belongs to God and that God is responsible for all creation, would, they hoped, assure God's blessing of fertility. God would make everything holy, they hoped, if they made their first fruits holy by offering them to God.

## Making Time Holy

### The Sabbath (Exod. 20:8, 11)

> (8) Remember the sabbath day, and keep it holy. . . . (11) For in six days the LORD made heaven and earth, the sea, and all that is in them, but rested the seventh day; therefore the LORD blessed the sabbath day and consecrated it.

The seventh day is sabbath, which is holy time, separated time. The text directs the Israelites to observe the sabbath in memory of creation. Each week, after working for six days, they were to refrain from work, thus honoring the day that God had blessed, consecrated, and made holy.

### Festivals of Passover and Unleavened Bread, First Fruits and Weeks (Lev. 23:4-6, 9-11, 15-16)

> (4) These are the appointed festivals of the LORD, the holy convocations, which you shall celebrate at the time appointed for them.

In addition to the sabbath day, the seventh day of each week, the Israelites are directed here to celebrate certain festivals at separated special times for the people to come together, separated from others, as God's holy people.

> (5) In the first month, on the fourteenth day of the month, at twilight, there shall be a passover offering to the LORD, (6) and on the fifteenth day of the same month is the festival of unleavened bread to the LORD; seven days you shall eat unleavened bread.

One of the Israelites' special feasts is Passover, occurring annually from twilight to twilight, between the fourteenth and fifteenth day of the first month. Combined with Passover is the feast of unleavened bread, celebrated on the fifteenth day of the same month. The feast celebrates the deliverance of the Israelites from bondage.

> (9) The LORD spoke to Moses: (10) Speak to the people of Israel and say to them: When you enter the land that I am giving you and you reap its harvest, you shall bring the sheaf of the first fruits of your harvest to the priest. (11) He shall raise the sheaf before the LORD, that you may find acceptance; on the day after the sabbath the priest shall raise it.

Harvest festivals constitute another opportunity to celebrate God's action on Israel's behalf. Dependent on the produce of the fields for animal and human food, and therefore for survival, the Israelites offer the first products of the field to God as an assertion of God's role in the land's fertility. The sheaf of the first fruits goes to the priest, who raises it before God; the people thus seek God's favor. The festival is holy time, an acknowledgment of God, thanksgiving for God's blessings, and joyful celebration for the much-appreciated harvest.

(15) And from the day after the sabbath, from the day on which you bring the sheaf of the elevation offering, you shall count off seven weeks; they shall be complete. (16) You shall count until the day after the seventh sabbath, fifty days; then you shall present an offering of new grain to the LORD.

In addition to the holy times of sabbath, Passover, the feast of unleavened bread, and the harvest festival, the festival of weeks provides another holy time, celebrated seven weeks after the harvest festival. As the feast of first fruits opens the harvest season, this festival, at which new grain is offered to God, formally closes it. Again, the people acknowledge their dependence on God for the land's fertility, food, and survival.

### The Festival of Trumpets, the Day of Atonement, and the Festival of Booths (Lev. 23:23-28, 33-36)

(23) The LORD spoke to Moses, saying: (24) Speak to the people of Israel, saying: In the seventh month, on the first day of the month, you shall observe a day of complete rest, a holy convocation commemorated with trumpet blasts. (25) You shall not work at your occupations; and you shall present the LORD's offering by fire.

Israel's holy time was carefully structured throughout the year. This text directs the people, on the first day of the seventh month, to observe a day of complete rest and a holy assembly, marked by trumpet blasts. No work was to take place, and they were to make burnt offerings to God.

(26) The LORD spoke to Moses, saying: (27) Now, the tenth day of this seventh month is the day of atonement; it shall be a holy convocation for you: you shall deny yourselves and present the LORD's offering by fire; (28) and you shall do no work during that entire day; for it is a day of atonement, to make atonement on your behalf before the LORD your God.

Nine days after the festival of trumpets the Israelites observed a day of atonement. Like other sacred time it was to be observed by abstention from work, by a holy assembly, and by burnt sacrifices.

In contrast to other feasts, however, this day was to be spent in self-denial atoning for unfaithfulness.

> (33) The LORD spoke to Moses, saying: (34) Speak to the people of Israel, saying: On the fifteenth day of this seventh month, and lasting seven days, there shall be a festival of booths to the LORD. (35) The first day shall be a holy convocation; you shall not work at your occupations. (36) Seven days you shall present the LORD's offerings by fire; on the eighth day you shall observe a holy convocation and present the LORD's offerings by fire; it is a solemn assembly; you shall not work at your occupations.

Five days after the day of atonement, and lasting for seven days, the Israelites celebrated a festival of booths. On the first day, as with many other feasts, the Israelites refrained from work and met in assembly. Each day the Israelites made burnt offerings. On the eighth day, they refrained again from work, came together, and presented burnt offerings to the Lord. Each festival turns ordinary time into sacred time, set aside to articulate aspects of Israel's covenant relationship with God.

### Making People Holy
*Leviticus 11:45; 19:2; 20:7-8, 26*

> (11:45) For I am the LORD who brought you up from the land of Egypt, to be your God; you shall be holy, for I am holy.

Here the Lord is identified as the deliverer of the people, who were in bondage in Egypt when the Lord brought them out. But deliverance is only part of the story. The Lord who delivered them became their God. Because God is holy, they, like God, are to be holy.

> (19:2) Speak to all the congregation of the people of Israel and say to them: You shall be holy, for I the LORD your God am holy.

The text directs Moses to speak to the Israelites and to guide them toward holiness. They are to be holy because the Lord, their God, is holy.

> (20:7) Consecrate yourselves therefore, and be holy; for I am the Lord your God. (8) Keep my statutes, and observe them; I am the Lord; I sanctify you.

Continuing to carry out the Lord's instruction, Moses tells the people to make themselves sacred and holy, because God is their Lord. God directs the people to obey the Lord's teachings; God will make the people holy.

> (20:26) You shall be holy to me; for I the Lord am holy, and I have separated you from the other peoples to be mine.

The Lord declares that the people will be set apart, that God is set apart and has set them apart from other peoples. Like God who is holy, the people will be holy.

### Making Space Holy
### Deuteronomy 23:14

> Because the Lord your God travels along with your camp, to save you and to hand over your enemies to you, therefore your camp must be holy, so that he may not see anything indecent among you and turn away from you.

Due to the holiness of God, God instructs the Israelites, through Moses, to keep their dwelling space holy. God travels with the people; God saves them; God brings them victory over enemies. As a corollary, and lest God depart from them, the people are to behave appropriately—with uprightness and decency.

### Leviticus 19:30

> You shall keep my sabbaths and reverence my sanctuary: I am the Lord.

Not only is Israel's camp to be holy because of God's presence, the Lord's sanctuary is holy by virtue of its being the Lord's sanctuary. The people are to behave appropriately, which means reverencing the sanctuary.

### Deuteronomy 12:5-7

> (5a) But you shall seek the place that the LORD your God will choose out of all your tribes as his habitation to put his name there.

In Deuteronomy, Moses refers repeatedly to "the place that the Lord will choose to put his name," once the Israelites have entered the land the Lord promised. Most likely this text was produced during the monarchy, in order to solidify the centrality of Israel's temple.

> (5b) You shall go there, (6) bringing there your burnt offerings and your sacrifices, your tithes and your donations, your votive gifts, your freewill offerings, and the firstlings of your herds and flocks. (7) And you shall eat there in the presence of the LORD your God, you and your households together, rejoicing in all the undertakings in which the LORD your God has blessed you.

To the temple in Jerusalem the Israelites were instructed to bring sacrificial offerings, votive offerings, freewill offerings, moneys, and offerings of the firstborn. All people were to eat in the presence of God, rejoicing because God had blessed them. This sacred and holy temple was to be the central, if not the exclusive, site of the covenant people's ritual encounter with God.

## Doing Justice

### God's Justice

### Deuteronomy 10:17-18

> (17) For the LORD your God is God of gods and LORD of lords, the great God, mighty and awesome, who is not partial and takes no bribe, (18) who executes justice for the orphan and the widow, and who loves the strangers, providing them food and clothing.

Moses describes God as the God of gods, before all other gods. God is Lord of lords, before all other lords. God is great, inspires awe, does not play favorites, and does not bargain. On the contrary, God acts justly on behalf of society's less powerful, including the child without a father, the wife whose husband has died, and the stranger. God provides food and clothing to meet their needs.

### Deuteronomy 32:36

> Indeed the LORD will vindicate his people, have compassion on his servants, when he sees that their power is gone, neither bond nor free remaining.

This verse occurs within Moses' farewell song. Describing Israel's infidelity to God and its punishment, the poem promises that God will remain faithful. When God's people have lost their power then God will have compassion. Consistent with God's justice, God will provide for the less powerful and the needy.

### Judges' Justice
### Deuteronomy 1:16-17a

> (16) I charged your judges at this time: "Give the members of your community a fair hearing, and judge rightly between one person and another, whether citizen or resident alien."

The description of a judge requires that he possess fairness and right judgment, and that he not discriminate.

> (17a) "You must not be partial in judging; hear out the small and the great alike; you shall not be intimidated by anyone, for the judgment is God's."

The text directs the judge to render impartial judgment based on the data of the case, not on the status of those bringing it to him. His judgment is not to be influenced inappropriately, nor is it to be swayed by threats and fear. Since judgment ultimately resides with God, those who act as judges are to judge as God would judge.

*Deuteronomy 16:18-20*

> (18) You shall appoint judges and officials throughout your tribes, in all your towns that the LORD your God is giving you, and they shall render just decisions for the people.

According to the Pentateuch, Israel's legal system was comprised in part of judges and lesser officials who were to render just judgment.

> (19) You must not distort justice; you must not show partiality; and you must not accept bribes, for a bribe blinds the eyes of the wise and subverts the cause of those who are in the right. (20) Justice, and only justice, you shall pursue, so that you may live and occupy the land that the LORD your God is giving you.

Judges were by no means to distort justice. They were not to show partiality in their judgments and were not to accept payment that might persuade them in one way rather than another. Bribes blind people to the truth and hinder the execution of just judgments. In contrast to such dishonesty, judges are to pursue one thing, and one thing alone: justice. Only then will they and the Lord's people be blessed.

## People's Justice

*Leviticus 19:15*

> You shall not render an unjust judgment; you shall not be partial to the poor or defer to the great; with justice you shall judge your neighbor.

Israel's God was a just God who acted justly. In like fashion Israel's judges were to act justly and to render just judgments. The people themselves were to behave similarly. It was wrong to render an unjust judgment, wrong to discriminate against the poor; it was wrong to favor persons of status and influence. Rather, one should judge justly.

*Deuteronomy 24:17; 25:13-15*

> (24:17) You shall not deprive a resident alien or an orphan
> of justice; you shall not take a widow's garment in pledge.

Justice demands the practice of certain behaviors and the avoidance of others. Deut. 24:17 demands just treatment for the child without a living father and the resident alien. Justice demanded that they not be taken advantage of. Nor was it right to deprive the poor or vulnerable of their garment (e.g., Exod. 22:25; Amos 2:8), never mind the widow. Widows, deprived of husbands and the livelihood husbands were responsible to provide, were also deprived of the possibility of conceiving children who could provide for them in the future. In the patriarchal culture of ancient Israel, widowhood most likely would have deprived a woman of a male intercessor in the town square or court. Without an intermediary, she was potential prey for the powerful and lacked protection against the greedy (see 2 Kings 4:1-7).

> (25:13) You shall not have in your bag two kinds of weights,
> large and small. (14) You shall not have in your house two
> kinds of measures, large and small. (15) You shall have only
> a full and honest weight; you shall have only a full and hon-
> est measure, so that your days may be long in the land that
> the LORD your God is giving you.

Justice demands that items be measured honestly, that weights render accurate information and not deceive. The prophet Amos describes calculated deception regarding the relationship between the amount to be weighed and the price paid (see Amos 8:5). The issues are deceit and theft, which are clearly condemned. Regardless of whether one type of measure was used for the wealthy and another type for the poor, duplicity is wrong. Only just behavior will receive the Lord's blessings of long life in the land promised.

# Showing Reverence for God

## *Rejecting Idols*

### *Exodus 20:23*

> You shall not make gods of silver alongside me, nor shall you make for yourselves gods of gold.

This directive is made and reinforced many times throughout the Pentateuch. Here, succinctly, the Israelites are prohibited from making gods from created matter—in this case silver and gold—which would stand beside, that is, in addition to, their covenant God. Israel's god was not a god among gods, such that Israel belonged to Yahweh and Canaan to Baal. Nor was Israel's god merely a god greater than other gods—like Dagon, only greater (see 1 Samuel 4–6). The Israelites came to understand their god as the only god. As such, while other peoples made nongods out of material substance, Israel's god could not be contained or even represented in the "work of men's hands."

### *Exodus 23:24*

> You shall not bow down to their gods, or worship them, or follow their practices, but you shall utterly demolish them and break their pillars in pieces.

Not only are the Israelites forbidden to make gods for themselves, they are forbidden to acknowledge gods whom other peoples have made. The Israelites cannot worship these gods, but are to worship the God who brought them out of Egypt. They cannot follow the practices of these gods, including, for example, human sacrifice. Rather, they are to destroy these gods. And if these gods can be destroyed by the Israelites, what kind of gods are they? Implied is that these gods are no gods, no more than human fabrications. In contrast, the Israelites' god is *the* god, not contained in a pillar that can be broken into pieces, but a god with power and who has demonstrated that power on Israel's behalf. It would make no sense for the Israelites to conform their behavior to the practices of a people who worship a pillar; the Israelites are to conform to the directives of their God, according to their covenant identity. Worship and practice walk hand in hand.

### Making a Sanctuary
*Exodus 25:1-8*

> (1) The LORD said to Moses: (2) Tell the Israelites to take for me an offering; from all whose hearts prompt them to give you shall receive the offering for me. (3) This is the offering that you shall receive from them: gold, silver, and bronze, (4) blue, purple, and crimson yarns and fine linen, goats' hair, (5) tanned rams' skins, fine leather, acacia wood, (6) oil for the lamps, spices for the anointing oil and for the fragrant incense, (7) onyx stones and gems to be set in the ephod and for the breastpiece. (8) And have them make me a sanctuary, so that I may dwell among them.

In this instance reverencing God is not expressed negatively—as in rejecting idols—but positively in the construction of a sanctuary. Moreover, in contrast to the directive to reject idols, this directive assumes the tone of a request. Only those who are willing, who want to, need participate. The offering the Lord suggests is not specific like offerings for other occasions or purposes. These offerings are volunteered and can include the following items: metals, yarns, linen, hair from goats, skins from rams, leather, wood, oil, spices, and precious stones. The people are told to use the gifts as contributions toward the making of a dwelling place for the Lord. God has given all that they have—creation; they give back to God from the gifts that God has given them to provide a sacred space for God as a dwelling place. The donated items are valuable, as the God for whom the sanctuary will be provided deserves their best.

### Consecrating Priests and Levites
*Exodus 29:1-2*

> (1) Now this is what you shall do to them to consecrate them, so that they may serve me as priests. Take one young bull and two rams without blemish, (2) and unleavened bread, unleavened cakes mixed with oil, and unleavened

wafers spread with oil. You shall make them of choice wheat flour.

One way to express reverence for God is to designate ministers from among the people who would function as intermediaries between God and the people. These men would serve as priests, overseeing the ritual sacrifices that the people were to offer to God (burnt offerings, cereal offerings, freewill offerings, etc.). In order to set these men aside for ministry, they were made sacred. As part of the consecration ritual, fruits of the field and precious animals were offered to God.

### Exodus 29:10-11

(10) You shall bring the bull in front of the tent of meeting. Aaron and his sons shall lay their hands on the head of the bull, (11) and you shall slaughter the bull before the LORD, at the entrance of the tent of meeting.

One animal offered to God during the ritual of the consecration was a young bull. The close connection between the future priest and the young male animal is expressed by the laying on of hands. Note that future priests are identified as male descendants of Aaron. The priesthood was inherited by patrilineal descent.

### Exodus 29:15-16

(15) Then you shall take one of the rams, and Aaron and his sons shall lay their hands on the head of the ram, (16) and you shall slaughter the ram, and take its blood and dash it against all sides of the altar.

Dashing blood against the sides of the altar was common in sacrificial rituals intended to consecrate the human party, to create a covenant relationship, or to renew covenant faithfulness.

### Exodus 29:19-20

(19) You shall take the other ram; and Aaron and his sons shall lay their hands on the head of the ram, (20) and you

shall slaughter the ram, and take some of its blood and put it on the lobe of Aaron's right ear and on the lobes of the right ears of his sons, and on the thumbs of their right hands, and on the big toes of their right feet, and dash the rest of the blood against all sides of the altar.

After sacrificing the third animal—the second ram—blood would be placed on the future priests' right earlobes, on the thumbs of their right hands, and on the big toes of their right feet; the rest of the blood was to be dashed against the altar. The altar, signifying God's presence, claimed the priests as God's own. From head to foot the work of God's hands was God's.

### Exodus 29:21

Then you shall take some of the blood that is on the altar, and some of the anointing oil, and sprinkle it on Aaron and his vestments and on his sons and his sons' vestments with him; then he and his vestments shall be holy, as well as his sons and his sons' vestments.

Reciprocity is achieved with the sprinkling of blood and oil on the priests and on the clothing they will wear during ritual functions. The consecration ritual makes both the priests and their clothing holy, separated for God.

### Exodus 29:35

Thus you shall do to Aaron and to his sons, just as I have commanded you; through seven days you shall ordain them.

Consecration is a serious matter, for the priests' role is not to be taken lightly. The verses in Exodus 29 signify this fact by their detail and by extending the duration of the ritual to seven days. Such duration is reserved for only the most solemn feasts.

Whether Israel's priests during the exile or others at an uncertain date produced these texts matters less than the texts' clear assertion that the persons associated with God's dwelling place and the sacrifices were, by that very fact, to be separated from others. Ritual provided part of the preparation for their sacred role and function.

## *Making Nazirite Vow and Other Vows*
### *Numbers 6:1-8*

> (1) The LORD spoke to Moses, saying: (2) Speak to the
> Israelites and say to them: When either men or women
> make a special vow, the vow of a nazirite, to separate them-
> selves to the LORD, (3) they shall separate themselves from
> wine and strong drink; they shall drink no wine vinegar or
> other vinegar, and shall not drink any grape juice or eat
> grapes, fresh or dried. (4) All their days as nazirites they
> shall eat nothing that is produced by the grapevine, not even
> the seeds or the skins.

Both men and women could make the vow of the Nazirite,
which would separate them to the Lord for a specific time. This
separation to the Lord was to manifest itself externally. They were
to separate themselves *from* wine, strong drink, wine vinegar,
other vinegar, grape juice, and grapes. By so doing, they separated
themselves *from* other Israelites for whom those items were quite
acceptable. Abstinence from these drinks and from grapes was to
last for the duration of the vow.

> (5) All the days of their nazirite vow no razor shall come
> upon the head; until the time is completed for which they
> separate themselves to the LORD, they shall be holy; they
> shall let the locks of the head grow long.

As an additional sign of separation to the Lord, Nazirites were
not to cut their hair for the duration of their vow. They were to be
holy, set apart for the Lord. Allowing hair to grow functioned as a
symbol and external manifestation of this separation.

> (6) All the days that they separate themselves to the LORD
> they shall not go near a corpse. (7) Even if their father or
> mother, brother or sister, should die, they may not defile
> themselves; because their consecration to God is upon the
> head. (8) All their days as nazirites they are holy to the LORD.

Since contact with a dead body rendered a person unclean,
Nazirites were to refrain from such contact. Touching the body of
a dead person would prevent them from entering the sanctuary

for prayer or sacrifice. Being set apart for God made it inappropriate for them to have such contact, even with the dead body of a family member. As persons consecrated to the Lord they were to be holy.

*Numbers 6:13-17*

> (13) This is the law for the nazirites when the time of their consecration has been completed: they shall be brought to the entrance of the tent of meeting, (14) and they shall offer their gift to the LORD, one male lamb a year old without blemish as a burnt offering, one ewe lamb a year old without blemish as a sin offering, one ram without blemish as an offering of well-being, (15) and a basket of unleavened bread, cakes of choice flour mixed with oil and unleavened wafers spread with oil, with their grain offering and their drink offerings. (16) The priest shall present them before the Lord and offer their sin offering and burnt offering, (17) and shall offer the ram as a sacrifice of well-being to the LORD, with the basket of unleavened bread; the priest also shall make the accompanying grain offering and drink offering.

As certain practices were associated with the time during which a person was a Nazirite, rituals also were associated with the ending of the vow. These involved a burnt offering, sin offering, offering of well-being, grain offerings, drink offerings, unleavened bread, cakes, and unleavened wafers. Unshorn hair was cut and then burned under the sacrifice of well-being. Part of the sacrifice of well-being—the shoulder, the breast, and the thigh of the ram as well as one unleavened wafer—constituted an elevation offering, the priest's portion of the sacrifice. After the offering was completed, the Nazirite was allowed to drink wine. A person taking the Nazirite vow had to conform to its rituals, though he or she was not prevented from adding more to the offering. Num. 6:21 suggests that other vows were made to God, with other associated signs and rituals. The verse directs that those who take a particular vow comply with the practices—the signs and rituals—associated with the vow they make.

## Maintaining Purity

Anthropologists suggest that cleanliness laws may have as much to do with establishing order in a society as they do with cleanliness itself. That may very well be the case. Nevertheless, the texts connect cleanliness with godliness and with human efforts to reverence God.

### Animals and Fish (Lev. 11:1-3, 9)

(1) The LORD spoke to Moses and Aaron, saying to them:
(2) Speak to the people of Israel, saying:
  From among the land animals, these are the creatures that you may eat. (3) Any animal that has divided hoofs and is cleft-footed and chews the cud—such you may eat. . . .
  (9) These you may eat, of all that are in the waters. Everything in the waters that has fins and scales, whether in the seas or in the streams—such you may eat.

If God is holy, and if the people, like God, are to be holy, then it stands to reason that even what the people eat should be carefully monitored. Among possible sources of food, are there foods that are better, healthier, and safer than others? Should there be no discrimination? God is not any god but their God, the only God. God has chosen the people and has set them apart. God has provided animals, with some serving as food, but can all provide food? Are some animals set apart for people who have been set apart? Are some fish set apart for people who have been set apart?

In answering these questions the text contributes to the ordering of the Israelites' lives. Those animals that have divided hoofs the Israelites may eat; implicitly, those animals that do not have divided hoofs they may not eat. The Israelites may eat cleft-footed animals and animals that chew the cud, but not animals that are not cleft-footed and that do not chew the cud. (With regard to aquatic life, Israelites may eat fish with fins and scales, but not fish without them.) What of animals that have one of these characteristics but not all three? Specifics follow the verses cited above. It is not enough to have one of these characteristics. All three characteristics are necessary to make the animal fit as food. Chewing the cud is not sufficient to make an animal, if it does not have divided hoofs, appropriate for eating. Likewise, having divided hoofs and cleft feet is not sufficient if the animal does not chew the cud.

### Women (Lev. 12:1-2, 4-8)

(1) The LORD spoke to Moses, saying: (2) Speak to the people of Israel, saying:

If a woman conceives and bears a male child, she shall be ceremonially unclean seven days; as at the time of her menstruation, she shall be unclean. . . . (4) Her time of blood purification shall be thirty-three days; she shall not touch any holy thing, or come in to the sanctuary, until the days of her purification are completed.

In ancient Israel blood was viewed both negatively and positively. Depending on what kind of blood it was, how it was used, and what it touched, it could pollute or purify. For example, whereas animal blood used in sacrifices was understood as a purifying agent, animal blood when eaten or when sprinkled on a priest's garment had a defiling effect. Human lifeblood could also either purify or pollute. A murder victim's blood polluted while a murderer's blood purified.

The blood flowing from a woman's body during menstruation or after childbirth was understood, in the patriarchal culture of ancient Israel, as polluting; it rendered the woman unclean. Perhaps this was because men feared and wished to control women's bodies. Perhaps the odor emitted and the need for washing contributed to the judgment. Whatever the reason, menstruating women or women discharging the placenta after childbirth were considered, during the time of the emission or expulsion of blood, unclean. Only after a stated period of time did they lack the potential to contaminate; again, only after a period of purification were they determined fit to enter the presence of God. Respect and reverence for God demanded that nothing impure or unclean should come before the Lord.

(5) If she bears a female child, she shall be unclean two weeks, as in her menstruation; her time of blood purification shall be sixty-six days.

If she has borne a female child, the time of a mother's uncleanness doubles. Again, although produced in a patriarchal culture in
which women were valued less than men, the verse simply accentuates that the female person born will herself emit and expel blood.

> (6) When the days of her purification are completed,
> whether for a son or for a daughter, she shall bring to the
> priest at the entrance of the tent of meeting a lamb in its
> first year for a burnt offering, and a pigeon or a turtledove
> for a sin offering. (7) He shall offer it before the LORD, and
> make atonement on her behalf; then she shall be clean from
> her flow of blood. This is the law for her who bears a child,
> male or female.

Having borne a child, its mother shall present the child to God.
In the child's place the priest will offer a lamb, which the woman
provides, as a burnt offering. As a purification offering, the priest
shall offer the pigeon or turtledove, which the woman also brings.
Passage of time combined with the sacrifice will purify the woman
from the uncleanness produced by the blood.

> (8) If she cannot afford a sheep, she shall take two turtle-
> doves or two pigeons, one for a burnt offering and the other
> for a sin offering; and the priest shall make atonement on
> her behalf, and she shall be clean.

If showing reverence for God is the ultimate purpose of the sacrifices and the entire ritual, then the God who instructs Israel to
provide for the poor will also provide. The woman who cannot
afford a lamb is not required to offer one. Rather, she can bring a
pigeon or a turtledove in its place. The directive thus implies the
acceptance of lesser offerings from the impoverished; the Lord
does not desire a sacrifice that will further impoverish the person
making the offering. By offering what one can, one shows reverence to God.

### Sufferers of Skin Diseases (Lev. 13:1-3, 14-15, 18-20, 24-25, 45-46)

> (1) The LORD spoke to Moses and Aaron, saying:
> (2) When a person has on the skin of his body a swelling
> or an eruption or a spot, and it turns into a leprous disease

on the skin of his body, he shall be brought to Aaron the priest or to one of his sons the priests. (3) The priest shall examine the disease on the skin of his body, and if the hair in the diseased area has turned white and the disease appears to be deeper than the skin of the body, it is a leprous disease; after the priest has examined him he shall pronounce him ceremonially unclean.

A person who is determined to have a skin disease shall be declared by the priest ceremonially unclean, that is, unfit to partake in ritual.

Despite the NRSV's translation and footnote, the English word *leprosy* identifies a single disease: Hansen's disease *(Mycobacterium leprae)*. The Bible, however, identifies a wide variety of skin ailments—some acute, some chronic—with a variety of visual features, conditions that we would diagnose as general infection, ringworm, rashes, psoriasis, boils, and so forth. Medical anthropologists claim that Hansen's disease was unknown or extremely rare in the ancient Near East.

(14) But if raw flesh ever appears on him, he shall be unclean; (15) the priest shall examine the raw flesh and pronounce him unclean. Raw flesh is unclean, for it is a leprous disease.

Just as swelling or an eruption or spot on the skin that is deeper than the surface and that turns the hair white indicates a skin disease, raw flesh can also serve as a sign. In any of these cases, the person who possesses the disease is unclean.

(18) When there is on the skin of one's body a boil that has healed, (19) and in the place of the boil there appears a white swelling or a reddish-white spot, it shall be shown to the priest. (20) The priest shall make an examination, and if it appears deeper than the skin and its hair has turned white, the priest shall pronounce him unclean; this is a leprous disease, broken out in the boil.

A boil that has healed but that is replaced by a white swelling or a reddish-white spot that is more than skin deep can also indicate a skin ailment, and that the person is unclean.

> (24) Or, when the body has a burn on the skin and the raw flesh of the burn becomes a spot, reddish-white or white, (25) the priest shall examine it. If the hair in the spot has turned white and it appears deeper than the skin, it is a leprous disease; it has broken out in the burn, and the priest shall pronounce him unclean. This is a leprous disease.

These verses represent repetition with variation. A burn that has caused the skin to become raw, and that becomes a reddish-white or white spot, also indicates a skin disease, if the hair on the spot has turned white. The person with such a burn has a skin ailment and is unclean.

> (45) The person who has the leprous disease shall wear torn clothes and let the hair of his head be disheveled; and he shall cover his upper lip and cry out, "Unclean, unclean." (46) He shall remain unclean as long as he has the disease; he is unclean. He shall live alone; his dwelling shall be outside the camp.

After describing the most common manifestations of skin disease, the text instructs infected persons regarding their behavior. They are to identify themselves as unclean and to make their appearance resemble the appearance of a person in mourning. Since the disease is potentially contagious, they are to dwell outside the camp and sleep alone.

These details all contribute to the bottom line: a person with a serious and contagious skin condition is ritually unclean. It is unlikely that all these skin diseases were leprosy, and what the ancients understood about leprosy remains unclear; nevertheless, it is clear that these bodily imperfections made a person less fit to appear before the Lord. Showing reverence to the Lord meant that, ideally, one came before the Lord with a "whole" and "undamaged" body.

### Men with a Discharge (Lev. 15:1-3)

> (1) The Lord spoke to Moses and Aaron, saying: (2) Speak to the people of Israel and say to them:

When any man has a discharge from his member, his discharge makes him ceremonially unclean. (3) The uncleanness of his discharge is this: whether his member flows with his discharge, or his member is stopped from discharging, it is uncleanness for him.

As the flow of blood renders a woman unclean, the discharge of semen has the same effect on a man. The discharge itself is not unclean, but the man with the discharge must be cleansed before he can appear before the Lord. To observe this teaching is to show reverence for the Lord.

### Priests (Lev. 21:6, 16-23)

(6) They [the priests] shall be holy to their God, and not profane the name of their God; for they offer the Lord's offerings by fire, the food of their God; therefore they shall be holy.

To show reverence for the Lord, it is only fitting that the very person of the priest must be holy, separated from the rest of the people. It is he who offers sacrifices to the Lord.

(16) The Lord spoke to Moses, saying: (17) Speak to Aaron and say: No one of your offspring throughout their generations who has a blemish may approach to offer the food of his God. (18) For no one who has a blemish shall draw near, one who is blind or lame, or one who has a mutilated face or a limb too long, (19) or one who has a broken foot or a broken hand, (20) or a hunchback, or a dwarf, or a man with a blemish in his eyes or an itching disease or scabs or crushed testicles. (21) No descendant of Aaron the priest who has a blemish shall come near to offer the Lord's offerings by fire; since he has a blemish, he shall not come near to offer the food of his God. (22) He may eat the food of his God, of the most holy as well as of the holy. (23) But he shall not come near the curtain or approach the altar, because he has a blemish, that he may not profane my sanctuaries; for I am the Lord; I sanctify them.

Because of their function to offer the Lord's sacrifices, priests must be holy out of reverence for God. Moreover, they must be without blemish. "Blemishes" include conditions such as blindness or lameness, or any other physical disability. The blemish detracts from the person who is to offer the Lord's sacrifices and thus renders him unfit.

The text does not blame the person with the blemish; indeed, the son of Aaron who possesses the blemish may still eat from even the most sacred of the ritual sacrifices. However, because of the blemish, he himself cannot offer the sacrifices.

Because the ancient Israelites did not understand the causes of certain physical diseases and disabilities, they understood disease and physical disformity as rendering one unfit to enter the presence of God or to serve as God's priest (e.g., Lev. 21:16-21). Because of the holiness of God, only the best of God's creation, including the best animals for sacrifice, should come before God. Israelites, because they identified health as a blessing, sometimes associated sickness with a curse. Nevertheless, as far as we know, they did not reject or ostracize those whose diseases or disabilities were known not to be contagious (see comments on Lev. 19:14 below).

## Persons Touching a Dead Body (Num. 19:10b-11)

(10b) This shall be a perpetual statute for the Israelites and for the alien residing among them. (11) Those who touch the dead body of any human being shall be unclean seven days.

Perhaps because God was associated with life, those who came into contact with the dead rendered themselves ritually unclean. The duration of their uncleanness was limited to seven days, and on the third and seventh days they were to undergo ritual cleansing. Failure to wash would extend the period of uncleanness; during their period of ritual uncleanness, out of reverence for God, they were not to enter the sanctuary. Failure to wash risked defiling the Lord's tabernacle.

# Showing Reverence for Others

## *Providing for and Protecting the Vulnerable*

### *The Stranger, the Widow, and the Fatherless (Exod. 22:21-22; 23:9)*

> (22:21) You shall not wrong or oppress a resident alien, for you were aliens in the land of Egypt. (22) You shall not abuse any widow or orphan.

Because of Israel's experience of bondage in Egypt, the people are directed not to wrong or oppress persons in a similar position. Having "been there," they are instructed not to treat others as they were treated. Moreover, other vulnerable persons in the patriarchal society—children without fathers or women whose husbands had died—were not to be turned into objects of abuse.

> (23:9) You shall not oppress a resident alien; you know the heart of an alien, for you were aliens in the land of Egypt.

This directive is reiterated frequently throughout the Pentateuch with the Israelites' experience as the motivation.

### *The Poor (Exod. 22:25; 23:3, 6)*

> (22:25) If you lend money to my people, to the poor among you, you shall not deal with them as a creditor; you shall not exact interest from them.

Material inequality was recognized, and often necessitated borrowing and lending. Borrowers, described here as those who were poorer than others, were not to be impoverished further by having to pay interest on loans; after all, they did not have the money in the first place. The directive was intended to prevent greater impoverishment and, in that way, to protect the poor.

> (23:3) . . . nor shall you be partial to the poor in a lawsuit.
> (6) You shall not pervert the justice due to the poor in their lawsuits.

Discrimination against the poor will not be tolerated in the legal system. Everyone, regardless of material possessions, should be treated impartially.

### Garments as Pledge (Exod. 22:26-27)

> (26) If you take your neighbor's cloak in pawn, you shall restore it before the sun goes down; (27) for it may be your neighbor's only clothing to use as cover; in what else shall that person sleep? And if your neighbor cries out to me, I will listen, for I am compassionate.

Assumed here is the legitimacy of taking another person's belongings because that person is indebted to you. Still, there are limits. One cannot take what the other person needs to survive or to stay healthy. A cloak that is borrowed must therefore be returned before the evening chill so the debtor can keep warm. If someone refuses or fails to return the cloak, and if the person deprived of his night's covering cries out to God (seemingly because of having to suffer from the cold and from the other's cruelty), God will take the side of the vulnerable person, the debtor.

An ostracon discovered near Yavneh-Yam on the Mediterranean coast, and dating between 639 and 609 B.C.E., contains a formal petition from a harvester whose garment had been taken several days before by a certain Hoshaiah ben-Shobai. In the document the speaker professes his innocence and asks the governor to intercede for the return of his garment.

Lev. 6:1-7 makes provision for a person who has sinned by "deceiving a neighbor in a matter of a deposit or a pledge," and who, having realized his guilt, wishes to restore the deposit that was "committed to" him. He is to offer an unblemished ram for a guilt offering. Dealing appropriately with garments taken in pledge was considered a serious matter.

### Slaves (Exod. 21:7-11)

> (7) When a man sells his daughter as a slave, she shall not go out as the male slaves do. (8) If she does not please her master, who designated her for himself, then he shall let her be redeemed; he shall have no right to sell her to a foreign people, since he has dealt unfairly with her.

In spite of the society's patriarchal character, certain provisions were in place to protect women. In this case, a daughter is distinguished from a son in that both can be sold as slaves, but the person purchasing a daughter cannot sell her to a foreign people. If the man who bought the woman rejects her, the law determines that he has dealt with her unfairly, for she had been sold with the understanding that she would belong to him.

> (9) If he designates her for his son, he shall deal with her as with a daughter.

The woman purchased as a wife/concubine for the buyer's son should not be treated as an object of purchase but as a daughter.

> (10) If he takes another wife to himself, he shall not diminish the food, clothing, or marital rights of the first wife.

After buying a woman who becomes his wife, a buyer may not cast her off or mistreat her if and when he chooses and/or buys another wife. The first woman deserves food, clothing, and marital rights, understood also as the continued opportunity to bear children.

> (11) And if he does not do these three things for her, she shall go out without debt, without payment of money.

Failure to provide properly for the woman purchased as a wife gives her the right to leave and owe nothing. In the patriarchal culture of ancient Israel, women, most likely the daughters of poorer males, could be purchased, but there were legal efforts within the patriarchal structure at least to protect their material well-being.

### The Deaf and the Blind (Lev. 19:14)

> You shall not revile the deaf or put a stumbling block before the blind; you shall fear your God: I am the LORD.

Although persons with physical disabilities were sometimes considered unclean, and disabled animals were not appropriate as sacrificial offerings, the law did protect those made vulnerable by their disabilities. Since deaf persons cannot defend themselves from verbal abuse, this directive protects them by forbidding others to speak against them. Similarly, the law forbids placing obstacles in the way of the blind, who might fall and hurt themselves. If "stumbling block" is interpreted symbolically (see, for example, Deut. 27:18), the law forbids *any* obstacle that might hinder a person already burdened with blindness.

### Seduction of a Virgin

Exodus 22:16-17

> (16) When a man seduces a virgin who is not engaged to be married, and lies with her, he shall give the bride-price for her and make her his wife. (17) But if her father refuses to give her to him, he shall pay an amount equal to the bride-price for virgins.

According to the provisions of this law, which is consistent with the patriarchal culture of ancient Israel, a man who seduced a virgin who was not yet engaged would not be punished for having had intercourse with her. He would, however, have had to (1) pay the bride-price for her, and (2) if the father would permit it, marry her. If the father was not willing to give up his daughter, the seducer would still have to pay the bride-price. Consequences result from irreverent actions toward other people—taking what does not belong to you, in this instance. Though the woman is seemingly left out of the decision making, the law provides that men cannot abuse other men's property and get away with it.

Deuteronomy 22:28-29

> (28) If a man meets a virgin who is not engaged, and seizes her and lies with her, and they are caught in the act, (29) the man who lay with her shall give fifty shekels of silver to the young woman's father, and she shall become his wife. Because he violated her, he shall not be permitted to divorce her as long as he lives.

The law provides that a man who takes a virgin who was not engaged at the time, and who then marries her, is not allowed to divorce her. The consequences for having violated her are meant to protect the woman's future, her material well-being, and her childbearing possibilities.

### A Person Guilty of Manslaughter
Exodus 21:12-13

> (12) Whoever strikes a person mortally shall be put to death. (13) If it was not premeditated, but came about by an act of God, then I will appoint for you a place to which the killer may flee.

Premeditated murder is here understood as deserving capital punishment. However, responsibility for a person's accidental death does not merit capital punishment. The law provides a place where the killer may flee.

Numbers 35:6a, 9-12

> (6a) The towns that you give to the Levites shall include the six cities of refuge, where you shall permit a slayer to flee. . . .
> (9) The LORD spoke to Moses, saying: (10) Speak to the Israelites, and say to them: When you cross the Jordan into the land of Canaan, (11) then you shall select cities to be cities of refuge for you, so that a slayer who kills a person without intent may flee there. (12) The cities shall be for you a refuge from the avenger, so that the slayer may not die until there is a trial before the congregation.

A person who kills another unintentionally does not deserve capital punishment. Yet it is possible, even likely, that the deceased person's next of kin will seek out the killer to avenge his dead relative. In order to prevent killing in revenge, the law provides for cities of refuge among the towns occupied by the levitical priests throughout the territory. At these places the person who has killed another unintentionally can find safety, at least until his guilt or innocence is determined.

### Helping One's Enemy
Exodus 23:4-5

> (4) When you come upon your enemy's ox or donkey going astray, you shall bring it back.

(5) When you see the donkey of one who hates you lying under its burden and you would hold back from setting it free, you must help to set it free.

Reverencing other people includes helping one's enemy. Verse 4 requires the performance of positive good for one's enemy, not just the avoidance of harm. One must return his stray animal to him. Verse 5 makes explicit that one must overcome the impulse not to get involved; one must act for the enemy's benefit, in this case by helping to free his overburdened donkey.

### Preserving Life

You shall not murder. (Exod. 20:13)
Anyone who kills a human being shall be put to death. (Lev. 24:17)
You shall not murder. (Deut. 5:17)

Generically put, these laws prohibit killing. While the Hebrew verb can be translated either "kill" or "murder," the NRSV translation prefers "murder," since situations exist in which killing is permitted, even commanded. (See, for example, Num. 35:16-21.)

### Deuteronomy 27:24-25

(24) "Cursed be anyone who strikes down a neighbor in secret." All the people shall say, "Amen!"
(25) "Cursed be anyone who takes a bribe to shed innocent blood." All the people shall say, "Amen!"

These curses condemn particularly heinous killings, those performed in secret and for a bribe. The first curse suggests that a murderer might remain unknown and, if not for the curse, unpunished. Verse 25 condemns the augmentation of one's material prosperity at the expense of human life.

### Being Honest

You shall not steal. (Exod. 20:15)
Neither shall you steal. (Deut. 5:19)

Reverencing other people includes not taking what rightfully belongs to them.

### Exodus 22:1-4

> (1) When someone steals an ox or a sheep, and slaughters it or sells it, the thief shall pay five oxen for an ox, and four sheep for a sheep. The thief shall make restitution, but if unable to do so, shall be sold for the theft. (4) When the animal, whether ox or donkey or sheep, is found alive in the thief's possession, the thief shall pay double.

Because taking what rightfully belongs to another person is wrong, provision is made for punishment. When one steals an ox or sheep and disposes of it, either by slaughter or sale, so that it cannot be returned, the law requires that the thief provide the rightful owner with five oxen or four sheep, depending on what was stolen originally. If the thief who has sold (or slaughtered) the animal cannot make restitution, then he himself is to be sold for restitution. If the stolen animal can be returned, the thief is to return it and to provide one more animal of the kind stolen. The provisions for punishment underline the seriousness of showing disregard for another human being by stealing property.

### Being Truthful

> You shall not bear false witness against your neighbor. (Exod. 20:16)
>
>  Neither shall you bear false witness against your neighbor. (Deut. 5:20)

Reverencing other people includes refraining from false testimony. An egregious example is recorded in 1 Kings 21, which tells of the death of Naboth, which was instigated by the evil Queen Jezebel but brought about because of the false testimony of two scoundrels.

*Exodus 23:1*

> You shall not spread a false report. You shall not join hands with the wicked to act as a malicious witness.

The law forbids the spreading of false rumors and also forbids complicity with others who wish to harm someone by rendering false testimony.

*Leviticus 19:11b-12,16a*

> . . . (11b) and you shall not lie to one another. (12) And you shall not swear falsely by my name, profaning the name of your God: I am the LORD.
> . . . (16a) You shall not go around as a slanderer among your people.

Reverencing other people includes telling the truth. The law forbids lying, especially lying while at the same time swearing by God's name to the truth of one's words. The law forbids saying falsehoods that have the potential to hurt others' reputations.

### Respecting Parents

> Honor your father and your mother, so that your days may be long in the land that the LORD your God is giving you. (Exod. 20:12)
> Honor your father and your mother, as the LORD your God commanded you, so that your days may be long and that it may go well with you in the land that the LORD your God is giving you. (Deut. 5:16)

The word *honor* in Hebrew derives from the word meaning to "make heavy" or "take seriously." Taking one's parents seriously, or honoring them, acknowledges their role in one's life and, as this teaching provides, secures for oneself a long life and well-being in the land.

*Exodus 21:15, 17*

> (15) Whoever strikes father or mother shall be put to death.
> (17) Whoever curses father or mother shall be put to death.

Because ancient Israelite society valued elders, including parents, and because one's parents make one's own life possible, treating a parent with contempt—striking or cursing one's father or mother—was deserving of death. One should show reverence to all, and to one's parents in particular. Failure to do so was a serious offense (see also Lev. 20:9).

### Respecting Sexual Identity and Relationships

> You shall not commit adultery. (Exod. 20:14)
> Neither shall you commit adultery. (Deut. 5:18)

Reverencing others includes not taking what is not available, and also includes not giving away what one does not own. Taking another man's rightful marriage partner was to act disrespectfully toward the rightful husband. A married woman belonged not to herself, moreover, but to her husband. For her then to sleep with another man was wrong. Both partners would have been engaging in adulterous behavior.

### Leviticus 18:6-18

> (6) None of you shall approach anyone near of kin to uncover nakedness: I am the LORD. (7) You shall not uncover the nakedness of your father, which is the nakedness of your mother; she is your mother, you shall not uncover her nakedness. (8) You shall not uncover the nakedness of your father's wife; it is the nakedness of your father. (9) You shall not uncover the nakedness of your sister, your father's daughter or your mother's daughter, whether born at home or born abroad. (10) You shall not uncover the nakedness of your son's daughter or of your daughter's daughter, for their nakedness is your own nakedness. (11) You shall not uncover the nakedness of your father's wife's daughter, begotten by your father, since she is your sister. (12) You shall not uncover the nakedness of your father's sister; she is your father's flesh. (13) You shall not uncover the nakedness of your mother's sister, for she is your mother's flesh. (14) You shall not uncover the nakedness of your father's brother, that is, you shall not approach

his wife; she is your aunt. (15) You shall not uncover the nakedness of your daughter-in-law: she is your son's wife; you shall not uncover her nakedness. (16) You shall not uncover the nakedness of your brother's wife; it is your brother's nakedness.

The law, which presupposes male heads of houses as its audience, prohibits incest—sexual relations with one's mother, the other wives of one's father, one's sister, one's granddaughter, one's aunt, one's daughter-in-law, or one's sister-in-law. One notes, however, that sons and daughters are not mentioned in this list; in all likelihood, this omission derives from the patriarchal assumption that no one could tell a father what he could do with his own children. But assuming the patriarchal culture of ancient Israel and consequent power relations, the observance of such a law could protect most female relatives from more powerful male predators within the family.

(17) You shall not uncover the nakedness of a woman and her daughter, and you shall not take her son's daughter or her daughter's daughter to uncover her nakedness; they are your flesh; it is depravity. (18) And you shall not take a woman as a rival to her sister, uncovering her nakedness while her sister is still alive.

The law provides further protection for women insofar as one man is not to engage in sexual relations with two women who are mother and daughter or mother and granddaughter, or with two sisters. The law is directed toward men, and insofar as it prevents the same man from marrying women who are related, it lessens the possibility of jealousy and rivalry, and is more likely to guarantee the women's material well-being.

## Repaying Damages
### Exodus 21:18-19

(18) When individuals quarrel and one strikes the other with a stone or fist so that the injured party, though not

dead, is confined to bed, (19) but recovers and walks around outside with the help of a staff, then the assailant shall be free of liability, except to pay for the loss of time, and to arrange for full recovery.

When one has hurt another, one takes responsibility for the action. In this case, one is to provide materially for the injured party during recovery—when the person cannot work—and further assists in the process of recovery.

## Exodus 22:5-6

(5) When someone causes a field or vineyard to be grazed over, or lets livestock loose to graze in someone else's field, restitution shall be made from the best in the owner's field or vineyard.

Again, reverencing other people includes taking responsibility for the injurious actions of one's animals. This verse directs the person whose animals have destroyed, at least temporarily, another person's property to make restitution from the best of his property, whether or not the damage was deliberate.

(6) When fire breaks out and catches in thorns so that the stacked grain or the standing grain or the field is consumed, the one who started the fire shall make full restitution.

Taking responsibility for one's actions—in this case, for starting a fire—means making full restitution, whether or not the injurious action was deliberate.

## Exodus 22:14

When someone borrows an animal from another and it is injured or dies, the owner not being present, full restitution shall be made.

In this instance, when borrowed property suffers damage or death while it is in the borrower's care, it is the borrower's responsibility to make restitution for the loss.

## Showing Reverence for All Life and All Things
### Deuteronomy 5:12-15

> (12) Observe the sabbath day and keep it holy, as the Lord your God commanded you. (13) Six days you shall labor and do all your work. (14) But the seventh day is a sabbath to the Lord your God; you shall not do any work—you, or your son or your daughter, or your male or female slave, or your ox or your donkey, or any of your livestock, or the resident alien in your towns, so that your male and female slave may rest as well as you. (15) Remember that you were a slave in the land of Egypt, and the Lord your God brought you out from there with a mighty hand and an outstretched arm; therefore the Lord your God commanded you to keep the sabbath day.

The passage depicts an integral working relationship among the Israelites, slaves, and animals. All, however, are to observe the sabbath. The reasoning is that male and female slaves, like the Israelites, need rest, as do the animals. Providing rest is a way of providing well-being.

The text assumes that the Israelites possessed slaves, though the circumstances under which people could become slaves in the ancient Near East were seemingly limited. They could be acquired as spoils of war—as lifetime prisoners of war, so to speak—or they could be born to slaves. Resident aliens could also become slaves, but not fellow Hebrews (see Lev. 25:39-46). All of Israel's slaves worked on behalf of the Israelites and were, accordingly, to receive rest each week.

### Deuteronomy 22:6-7

> (6) If you come on a bird's nest, in any tree or on the ground, with fledglings or eggs, with the mother sitting on the fledglings or on the eggs, you shall not take the mother with the young. (7) Let the mother go, taking only the young for yourself, in order that it may go well with you and you may live long.

The passage provides freedom for the mother bird again to produce eggs and fledglings. By releasing the mother one has not destroyed the source of life, only taken some of her offspring. One should not greedily take everything that one finds and can use. One should leave things for others or for tomorrow—manna, sheaves in the field, even birds.

### Deuteronomy 25:4

You shall not muzzle an ox while it is treading out the grain.

Cruelty to animals is not fitting; rather, it is appropriate to appreciate how animals work to human benefit, and to treat them accordingly.

Though Pentateuchal texts seem to give considerably more space and attention to the reverencing of God and humans than to the reverencing of other living beings, the reverencing of these living beings is required for humankind's welfare. Humankind will be the worse if plants and animals are not respected. Reverencing all living beings constitutes, then, an integral part of the ancient Near Eastern world from which the Bible comes. With a certain reciprocity, fields and animals that are treated reverently are more likely to produce with bounty.

# Conclusion

---

T HIS LIBERATION-CRITICAL READING OF THE Pentateuch is far from exhaustive. Many more passages could have been included for analysis and reflection. Some would merely repeat with slight variation the concerns presented here, while others would add nuances and further develop the thesis and thrust. Moreover, certain passages presented here could have been categorized under several headings, or could have been slanted differently to conform to another part of the book's conceptual structure. The conceptual structure itself is open to refinement. The effort is deliberately limited, seeking to suggest that there is more than one way to read biblical materials which, despite the patriarchal culture that produced them, are nonpatriarchal, nonhierarchical, and liberating.

This volume has tried to emphasize the dependence, implied by the texts, of human beings on other living beings, and the consequent interdependence of all living things. Because the peoples of the ancient world, including ancient Israel, experienced their dependence on nature more directly than those of us in First World countries at the turn of the millennium, placing these texts in historical context can be helpful in the search for valid interpretations. But such contextualization can especially help in the search for interpretations that seek to be nonpatriarchal, nonhierarchical, and liberating. Despite all the evidence of patriarchy and hierarchy in these biblical materials, the Pentateuch contains an integral strand that subverts, rejects, and condemns patriarchal and hierarchical ordering and that highlights relationships which are interdependent, covenantal, respectful, and reciprocal.

# Bibliography

T HE BIBLIOGRAPHY BELOW IS A *compilation of books that have been integral to this writing. In keeping with a liberation-critical methodology and the assertion of cosmic interdependence, I wish to acknowledge what is not included: many periodical, journal, and newspaper articles on far-ranging subjects, many conversations with women and men, many walks with my golden retriever Leah, and many trips to farms and to both lush and ravished countrysides. The human has privileged the printed, but a consciousness of our cosmic interdependence is more extensive than the written word.*

Ackerman, Diane. *The Moon by Whale Light and Other Adventures among Bats, Penguins, Crocodilians, and Whales.* New York: Vintage, 1991.

Armstrong, Karen. *The Gospel according to Woman: Christianity's Creation of the Sex War in the West.* Garden City, N.Y.: Anchor/Doubleday, 1987.

Bal, Mieke. *Lethal Love: Feminist Literary Readings of Biblical Love Stories.* Bloomington: Indiana University Press, 1987.

Bell, Derrick. *Faces at the Bottom of the Well: The Permanence of Racism.* New York: Basic Books, 1992.

Berry, Wendell. *The Unsettling of America: Culture and Agriculture.* San Francisco: Sierra Club Books, 1977.

Braude, Ann. *Radical Spirits: Spiritualism and Women's Rights in Nineteenth-Century America.* Boston: Beacon, 1989.

Brenner, Athalya. *The Israelite Woman: Social Role and Literary Type in Biblical Narrative.* Biblical Seminar, 2. Sheffield, England: JSOT Press, 1985.

——————, ed. *A Feminist Companion to the Hebrew Bible in the New Testament.* Feminist Companion to the Bible, 10. Sheffield, England: Sheffield Academic Press, 1996.

Bronner, Leila Leah. *From Eve to Esther: Rabbinic Reconstructions of Biblical Women.* Louisville: Westminster/John Knox, 1994.

Brown, Cheryl Anne. *No Longer Be Silent: First-Century Jewish Portraits of Biblical Women.* Louisville: Westminster/John Knox, 1992.

Carmody, Denise Lardner. *Seizing the Apple: A Feminist Spirituality of Personal Growth.* New York: Crossroad, 1984.

Cary, Lorene. *Black Ice.* New York: Vintage, 1991.

Cesaretti, C. A., and Stephen Commins. *Let the Earth Bless the Lord: A Christian Perspective on Land Use.* New York: Seabury, 1981.

Christ, Carol P. *Diving Deep and Surfacing: Women Writers on Spiritual Quest.* 2d. ed. Boston: Beacon, 1980.

Collins, Adela Yarbro, ed. *Feminist Perspectives on Biblical Scholarship.* Biblical Scholarship in North America, 10. Atlanta: Scholars Press, 1985.

Conn, Joann Wolski, ed. *Women's Spirituality: Resources for Christian Development.* New York: Paulist, 1986.

Cording, Robert. *What Binds Us to This World.* Providence, R.I.: Copper Beech, 1991.

Corrington, Gail Paterson. *Her Image of Salvation: Female Saviors and Formative Christianity.* Louisville: Westminster/John Knox, 1992.

Cunneen, Sally. *In Search of Mary: The Woman and the Symbol.* New York: Ballantine, 1996.

Darr, Katheryn Pfisterer. *Far More Precious Than Jewels: Perspectives on Biblical Women.* Gender and the Biblical Tradition. Louisville: Westminster/John Knox, 1991.

Donovan, Mary Ann, S.C. *Sisterhood as Power: The Past and Passion of Ecclesial Women*. New York: Crossroad, 1989.

Ellison, Ralph. *Invisible Man*. New York: Random House, 1952; 2d ed., New York: Vintage International, 1980.

Esposito, John L. *Women in Muslim Family Law*. Syracuse, N.Y.: Syracuse University Press, 1982.

Estés, Clarissa Pinkola. *Women Who Run with the Wolves: Myths and Stories of the Wild Woman Archetype*. New York: Ballantine, 1992.

Exum, J. Cheryl. *Fragmented Women: Feminist (Sub)Versions of Biblical Narratives*. Valley Forge, Pa.: Trinity Press International, 1993.

Ferguson, Marianne. *Women and Religion*. Englewood Cliffs, N.J.: Prentice-Hall, 1995.

Fiorenza, Elisabeth Schüssler. *Bread Not Stone: The Challenge of Feminist Biblical Interpretation*. Boston: Beacon, 1984.

——————. *But She Said: Feminist Practices of Biblical Interpretation*. Boston: Beacon, 1992.

——————. *In Memory of Her: A Feminist Theological Reconstruction of Christian Origins*. New York: Crossroad, 1983.

——————, ed. *Searching the Scriptures*. Vol. 2, *A Feminist Commentary*. New York: Crossroad, 1994.

Gerstenberger, Erhard S. *Yahweh the Patriarch: Ancient Images of God and Feminist Theology*. Minneapolis: Fortress Press, 1996.

Gold, Barbara K., Paul Allen Miller, and Charles Platter, eds. *Sex and Gender in Medieval and Renaissance Texts: The Latin Tradition*. Albany, N.Y.: SUNY Press, 1996.

Gregg, Joan Young. *Devils, Women, and Jews: Reflections on the Other in Medieval Sermon Stories*. Albany, N.Y.: SUNY Press, 1996.

Haizlip, Shirlee Taylor. *The Sweeter the Juice: A Family Memoir in Black and White*. New York: Simon & Schuster, 1994.

Hanson, K. C. "Blood and Purity in Leviticus and Revelation." *Listening: Journal of Religion and Culture* 28 (1993): 215–30.

Heschel, Susannah, ed. *On Being a Jewish Feminist: A Reader*. New York: Schocken, 1983.

Hinsdale, Mary Ann, and Phyllis H. Kaminski, eds. *Women and Theology.* The Annual Publication of the College Theology Society. Vol. 40. Maryknoll, N.Y.: Orbis Books, 1995.

Hollyday, Joyce. *Clothed with the Sun: Biblical Women, Social Justice, and Us.* Louisville: Westminster/John Knox, 1994.

Isasi-Diaz, Ada Maria, and Yolanda Tarango. *Hispanic Women: Prophetic Voice in the Church.* San Francisco: Harper & Row, 1988.

Kam, Rose Sallberg. *Their Stories, Our Stories: Women of the Bible.* New York: Continuum, 1995.

Kates, Judith A., and Gail Twersky Reimer, eds. *Reading Ruth: Contemporary Women Reclaim a Sacred Story.* New York: Ballantine, 1994.

Kenneally, James K. *The History of American Catholic Women.* New York: Crossroad, 1990.

Kingsolver, Barbara. *Pigs in Heaven.* New York: Harper Perennial, 1993.

Koltum, Elizabeth. *The Jewish Woman: New Perspectives.* New York: Schocken, 1976.

Krall, Florence. *Ecotone: Wayfaring on the Margins.* Albany, N.Y.: SUNY Press, 1996.

Kraemer, Ross Shepard. *Her Share of the Blessings: Women's Religions Among Pagans, Jews, and Christians in the Greco-Roman World.* New York: Oxford University Press, 1992.

Laffey, Alice L. *An Introduction to the Old Testament: A Feminist Perspective.* Philadelphia: Fortress Press, 1988.

Lemay, Helen Rodnite. *Women's Secrets: A Translation of Pseudo-Albertus Magnus' De Secretis Mulierum with Commentaries.* Albany, N.Y.: SUNY Press, 1996.

L'Engle, Madeleine. *Sold into Egypt: Joseph's Journey into Human Being.* Wheaton, Ill.: Harold Shaw Publishers, 1989.

Lerner, Gerda. *The Creation of Patriarchy.* New York: Oxford University Press, 1986.

Lesko, Barbara S., ed. *Women's Earliest Records from Ancient Egypt and Western Asia.* Atlanta: Scholars Press, 1989.

Levi, Primo. *The Drowned and the Saved.* New York: Vintage International, 1988.

──────────. *The Periodic Table.* New York: Schocken, 1984.

──────────. *Survival in Auschwitz.* New York: Simon & Schuster, 1996.

Mayeski, Marie Anne. *Women: Models of Liberation.* Kansas City, Mo.: Sheed & Ward, 1988.

McCourt, Frank. *Angela's Ashes: A Memoir.* New York: Scribner, 1996.

McFague, Sallie. *Models of God: Theology for an Ecological, Nuclear Age.* Philadelphia: Fortress Press, 1987.

McNamara, Jo Ann Kay. *Sisters in Arms: Catholic Nuns through Two Millennia.* Cambridge: Harvard University Press, 1996.

Meyers, Carol. *Discovering Eve: Ancient Israelite Women in Context.* New York: Oxford University Press, 1988.

Mollenkott, Virginia Ramey, ed. *Women of Faith in Dialogue.* New York: Crossroad, 1987.

Moyers, Bill. *Genesis: A Living Conversation.* New York: Doubleday, 1996.

Newsom, Carol A., and Sharon H. Ringe, eds. *The Women's Bible Commentary.* Louisville: Westminster/John Knox, 1992.

Nugent, Robert, and Jeannine Gramick. *Building Bridges: Gay and Lesbian Reality and the Catholic Church.* Mystic, Conn.: Twenty-Third Publications, 1992.

Nuland, Sherwin B. *How We Die: Reflections on Life's Final Chapter.* New York: Vintage, 1993.

Osiek, Carolyn, R.S.C.J. *Beyond Anger: On Being a Feminist in the Church.* New York: Paulist, 1986.

Pike, Christopher. *Sati.* New York: TOR, 1990.

Pixley, George V. *On Exodus: A Liberation Perspective.* Maryknoll, N.Y.: Orbis, 1987.

Plaskow, Judith. *Standing Again at Sinai: Judaism from a Feminist Perspective.* San Francisco: Harper & Row, 1990.

Ranke-Heinemann, Uta. *Eunuchs for the Kingdom of Heaven: Women, Sexuality, and the Catholic Church.* New York: Penguin, 1990.

Raspail, Jean. *The Camp of the Saints.* Petroskey, Mich.: The Social Contract Press. Original French publication, 1973.

Rose, Lois. *To Be Conscious: Meditations on Genesis, Exodus, and Job.* Stockbridge, Mass.: A Rose-Mark Meditation Book, 1993.

Ruether, Rosemary Radford. *New Woman New Earth: Sexist Ideologies and Human Liberation.* New York: Seabury, 1975.

—————. *Sexism and God-Talk: Toward a Feminist Theology.* Boston: Beacon, 1983.

—————. *Womanguides: Readings toward a Feminist Theology.* Boston: Beacon, 1985.

—————, ed. *Religion and Sexism: Images of Women in the Jewish and Christian Traditions.* New York: Simon & Schuster, 1974.

Ruether, Rosemary Radford, and Rosemary Skinner Keller, eds. *In Our Own Voices: Four Centuries of American Women's Religious Writing.* San Francisco: Harper SanFrancisco, 1995.

Ruether, Rosemary Radford, and Rosemary Skinner Keller, general editors. *Women and Religion in America.* Vol. 2, *The Colonial and Revolutionary Periods, A Documentary History.* San Francisco: Harper & Row, 1981.

Ruether, Rosemary Radford, and Eleanor McLaughlin, eds. *Women of Spirit: Female Leadership in the Jewish and Christian Traditions.* New York: Simon & Schuster, 1979.

Sacks, Oliver. *An Anthropologist on Mars.* New York: Vintage, 1995.

Shilts, Randy. *And the Band Played On: Politics, People, and the AIDS Epidemic.* New York: Penguin, 1988.

Schneiders, Sandra M. *Beyond Patching: Faith and Feminism in the Catholic Church.* New York: Paulist, 1991.

—————. *New Wineskins: Re-imaging Religious Life Today.* New York: Paulist, 1986.

—————. *Women and the Word.* New York: Paulist, 1986.

Schottroff, Luise. *Let the Oppressed Go Free: Feminist Perspectives on the New Testament.* Louisville: Westminster/John Knox, 1991.

Sewell, Marilyn, ed. *Cries of the Spirit: A Celebration of Women's Spirituality.* Boston: Beacon, 1991.

Soelle, Dorothee. *The Strength of the Weak: Toward a Christian Feminist Identity.* Trans. R. Kimber and R. Kimber. Philadelphia: Westminster, 1984.

Spretnak, Charlene. *Lost Goddesses of Early Greece: A Collection of Pre-Hellenic Myths.* Boston: Beacon, 1978.

Stanton, Elizabeth Cady. *The Woman's Bible.* New York: European Publishing Company, 1895–98; Boston: Northeastern University Press, 1993.

Stone, Merlin. *When God Was a Woman.* New York: Harcourt Brace Jovanovich, 1976.

Sugirtharajah, R. S., ed. *Voices from the Margin: Interpreting the Bible in the Third World.* Maryknoll, N.Y.: Orbis, 1991.

Swidler, Leonard, and Arlene Swidler, eds. *Women Priests: A Catholic Commentary on the Vatican Declaration.* New York: Paulist, 1977.

Tetlow, Elisabeth M. *Women and Ministry in the New Testament.* New York: Paulist, 1980.

Teubal, Savina J. *Hagar, the Egyptian: The Lost Tradition of the Matriarchs.* San Francisco: Harper & Row, 1990.

Thornton, Yvonne S., M.D., as told to Jo Coudert. *The Ditchdigger's Daughters: A Black Family's Astonishing Success Story.* New York: Plume, 1995.

Trible, Phyllis. *God and the Rhetoric of Sexuality.* Overtures to Biblical Theology. Philadelphia: Fortress Press, 1978.

——————. *Texts of Terror: Literary-Feminist Readings of Biblical Narratives.* Overtures to Biblical Theology. Philadelphia: Fortress Press, 1984.

Waetjen, Herman C. *A Reordering of Power: A Socio-Political Reading of Mark's Gospel.* Minneapolis: Fortress Press, 1989.

Ware, Ann Patrick, ed. *Midwives of the Future: American Sisters Tell Their Story.* Kansas City, Mo.: Leaven Press, 1985.

Weedon, Chris. *Feminist Practice and Poststructuralist Theory.* Oxford: Basil Blackwell, 1987.

Weems, Renita J. *Just a Sister Away: A Womanist Vision of Women's Relationships in the Bible.* San Diego: LuraMedia, 1988.

Weidman, Judith L., ed. *Christian Feminism: Visions of a New Humanity.* San Francisco: Harper & Row, 1984.

Wilson, Katharina M., and Elizabeth M. Makowski, eds. *Wykked Wyves and the Woes of Marriage: Misogamous Literature from Juvenal to Chaucer.* Albany, N.Y.: SUNY Press, 1996.

Wittberg, Patricia. *The Rise and Fall of Catholic Religious Orders: A Social Movement Perspective.* Albany, N.Y.: SUNY Press, 1994.

Wong, Mary Gilligan. *Nun: A Memoir.* New York: Harper Colophon, 1983.

# Index of Biblical References

# Index of Subjects

*In keeping with the book's focus, the index locates terms that describe cosmic inter-dependence: animals, plants, the nonhuman, and aspects of human beings that are shared with other animals. Named women are included. The index also lists words that express relationships that are interdependent and mutual. Some form of the term (e.g., plural, possessive, verbal) occurs on the page cited.*